Costing: A Management Approach

A. H. Taylor has had varied experience in the financial and marketing areas of a wide range of business and was Secretary and Chief Accountant of the UK subsidiary of a large American electronics corporation. He is now Course Director of the Business Studies degree course at the School of Business, Ealing, and manages to combine this appointment with selected consultancy work. He is the joint author, with R. E. Palmer, of *Financial Planning and Control*, also published in the Pan Management Series, amongst other publications on financial management.

Management Series

Costing: A Management Approach

A. H. TAYLOR, MC, FCCA

A PAN ORIGINAL

PAN BOOKS LTD : LONDON

First published 1974 by Pan Books Ltd,
33 Tothill Street, London SW1

ISBN 0 330 23822 1

Printed and bound in Great Britain by
Cox & Wyman Ltd, London, Reading and Fakenham

Contents

Preface

Costing is an essential function in a manufacturing company and well-developed systems of costing are to be found in industries as diverse as mining, farming, catering, transport, printing, public services, retail stores and professional practices. According to the needs and the nature of the organization, manufacturing costs may be expressed in terms of jobs, batches, processes and products. In transport the costing unit is frequently the ton mile, in farming the acre of land, in retail stores a measure of counter space. The variety of costing systems and methods is enormous and there can be few organizations in either the public or private sectors of the economy without some form of costing.

Because costing is so important to industry and commerce, it will be useful to consider its nature and objectives before examining the ways in which those objectives may be best achieved. The simplest description of costing is that it is the analysis of business expense. Thus the wage bill of a company is analysed by the costing system and allocated amongst the various jobs and operations carried out by the workers in a given period of time. Purchases of materials are analysed by types and then, when the material is consumed in the productive processes, re-analysed by jobs, operations, processes, etc. The overheads are analysed in various ways according to the requirements of the business and ultimately apportioned to products; apportionment being, in essence, a form of analysis.

The question which needs to be asked continually in any business where a costing system is installed is: What is the purpose of the system? One fundamental purpose is to assign a cost to the various items of work in progress and thence to the finished stock, so that when that stock is sold the cost is set off against the price obtained for it. In this way the management is able to study the relative profitability of the different categories of sales and thus to take such action as may be necessary to re-direct effort.

It is, however, the managers and not the accountant who are responsible for directing effort. The basic costing information indicated above must accordingly be directed to the managers although that information will also be necessary for the purpose of drawing up the final accounts.

The three basic elements in the achievement of profits are price, cost and volume; and these elements are interacting. Thus, price may be influenced by cost and volume of sales; cost will be influenced by volume; and volume will be influenced by price and capacity to produce. Where, as is the situation with many businesses, the capacity can be applied to a variety of products or services, a further vital consideration for management is to apply the capacity amongst the various products in the most efficient manner: in other words to achieve the optimum 'mix'. The job of the accountant is to provide the managers with the financial information they require for resolving all the factors affecting profitability. This information will need to go beyond the costing of the products and services for sale, and penetrate to the cost of the jobs, processes and operations from which the product cost is derived.

It is a truism that managers are concerned with controlling current performance and planning the future activities which fall within their responsibility. If the costs of last month's or last year's activities are guides to the future, then they are useful to managers; otherwise they can only be a matter for self-congratulation or remorse, neither of which is likely to assist current or future profitability. So far as forward planning is concerned, the essential job of the manager is to decide between alternative courses of action and to assign priorities. For these purposes he will require, for example, the cost of using different methods of working, of the alternative costs of making or buying out, of the effect of changes in volume on costs, and of changing the 'mix' of the products. These costs will be predictions, not historical facts.

Information needed by managers for the purposes of cost control need not be confined to the operations directly concerned with producing the goods or services for sale. A large, probably increasing proportion of business expenses is only remotely connected with the factory or other centre of direct operations. A pound saved in the office is as much a pound of additional profit as an equal saving in the works. The control of administrative and selling costs is an area somewhat neglected by the costing function, which has traditionally concentrated on manufacturing costs. It is probable that many businesses would derive great benefit from a rigorous examination of the cost of maintenance, the canteen, the typing and filing service and similar functions – even the cost of costing itself. Likewise useful information can often be obtained by watching the cost of various operations in the sales departments, such as the cost of calls made by salesmen, and the cost of taking and processing an order. These isolated examples are intended only to indicate the immense scope and potential of an active and alert costing service; but of course the expense of producing the information will be wasted if it is not required or not used.

The real danger in the production of cost information for management is that the figures may be presented as absolute and immutable quantities. Certainly the routine figures of product costs which emanate from the costing system are necessarily based on a number of conventions and assumptions. In charging material costs to jobs, for example, the accountant may decide to use the convention that the earliest purchases are the first used, or he may use the average price of the articles in stock, or some other convention. It is not possible to assert that one convention produces a more accurate cost than another; only to argue about the principles involved. What is more important is that the manager using the figures should understand the convention which is adopted. Likewise the accountant must make an assumption about the volume of future activity when he calculates the overhead rate to be applied to direct costs. This assumption may be falsified by events, and even if the assumption is correct the resultant 'full cost' is little more than the outcome of spreading business expenses over units of output. That 'full cost' will have only a very limited use for decision-making purposes; the cost of the product, and of each operation involved in producing the product, will be a variable quantity, depending on the use to be made of the figures.

This is not to suggest that the figures produced by the routine costing system are necessarily misleading or worthless. The purpose of that system is to value stock and work in progress as an essential element in the ascertainment of profit. In the process of ascertaining the profit made by a business in a period of, say, a year, it is necessary for the accountant to adopt certain conventions, as mentioned above, and, so far as is reasonable, to apply those conventions consistently year by year. The purpose of consistency is to produce accounts that will be comparable, period by period. The output of the routine costing system is not, therefore, designed primarily to provide information to managers for planning and control, except that presumably managers should be aware of the profitability of the whole enterprise, and of its constituent parts.

Even cost information prepared for managerial purposes will contain assumptions and conventions which will depend on the objectives of the exercise. Thus an inquiry as to the likely costs of additional output in order to ascertain the minimum price that could be quoted, involves an assumption as to volume, the duration of the additional output, and the overhead costs likely to be involved. If the managers are to draw valid conclusions from the information it is necessary that they should understand – and if necessary be prepared to criticize – the assumptions contained in the figures.

This is not a textbook on costing mechanics, although some references to customary techniques are included as a preliminary to an examination of their validity in the modern environment. The modest intention of this book is to examine the extent to which costing may be used to assist managers in their functions of forward planning and control.

1 The Meaning and Objectives of Costing

*What costing means; The objectives of costing;
Costing as an aid to forward planning; Cost and the
determination of price; The valuation of stocks and
work in progress*

What is 'costing'?

This chapter is frankly introductory. It attempts to define
the nature and purpose of costing within the framework of
a business organization. The justification for a preliminary
discussion of this nature, before getting down to the meat
and bones of the subject, is that under the pressures of
modern business, managers should be continually asking:
Why do we do this? What are the objectives? The fact that
a business has always had a costing system is no answer to
these questions.

Like so many of the more familiar terms used in business,
the word 'cost' can have a wide variety of meanings. When,
for example, we talk about the cost of, say, a chair which we
are proposing to buy for the home or the office, we are more
precisely referring to the price which we shall have to pay to
the retailer. In the eyes of the retailer the cost of the chair
will probably be the price he has had to pay the manufacturer for the article. To the manufacturer the cost of the
chair will have a very different meaning from that in the
mind of the retailer or of the ultimate buyer. In fact,
depending on the circumstances in which he uses the word,

the manufacturer may be referring to one of a number of possible ideas. He may, for example, be considering the costs incurred by his workshop in making the chair, or he may mean the workshop costs plus various additions for warehousing, distribution, selling and administrative expenses. He may be referring to the average costs of a production run of several hundred chairs, or the average costs last month or last year, the standard costs of making a chair under normal conditions, or perhaps the cost of making one more chair.

Some conclusions important to the present discussion can be derived from the foregoing. The first is that the words 'cost' and 'price' tend to be interchangeable unless we are careful to distinguish between these two distinct ideas. 'When I use a word it means just what I choose it to mean, neither more nor less'* was not a model formula for precise communication. The second point is that there is no such thing as *the* cost of an article; cost is not an absolute value but depends on the viewpoint and intentions of the person using the figure and the circumstances in which it is used.

In spite of the fact that the cost of an article or a service is variable according to circumstances and intentions, the *routine* costing system of a business is designed to produce one figure and one only to represent that cost. This is so because that costing system has as its primary purpose the objective of valuing the work in progress and the finished stock as part of the accounting process of ascertaining profit. For this purpose it is necessary to apply certain assumptions and a body of conventions in order to achieve a reasonably consistent view of profit. The routine costing system cannot, therefore, serve every purpose. It will almost always be necessary to interpret and usually to amend the output of the routine costing system to meet particular objectives. It will, furthermore, be essential for the managers who are using the system to understand the assumptions and conventions currently in use in that system.

The ultimate aim of the costing system, as such, is to arrive at the cost of the product or service for sale, given the

* Humpty Dumpty in *Through the Looking Glass.*

conventions and assumptions which must be implicit in the exercise. But the finished article is frequently the outcome of a large number of separate operations in the factory, and an equally large number of functions or operations are involved in the process of selling the product and in the administration of the business. The focal point of managerial control must, in consequence, lie with the cost of these operations and functions.

Cost is related to output and time

The outgoings incurred in a department of a business, or in the business as a whole, are collected in a financial ledger system under categories of expense, such as salaries and wages, employee benefits, premises occupation expense, maintenance, communications, finance charges, and so on. A broad form of control over departmental expense is operated through budgetary control, or perhaps simply by watching whether the expenses are rising or falling month by month. The fact, however, that in a particular period the departmental expenses exceed the budget is not in itself an indication of departmental inefficiency because during the period concerned the department may have carried out an increased work load. The existence of a budget variance will do little more than initiate inquiries as to the reasons for the excess spending.

A more incisive form of control begins with subdividing the department (whether it is in the works or administrative areas) into integral cost centres, such as a group of machines, a typing pool or an order-processing section. The next exercise is to calculate the unit cost of the work being done by dividing the expense by the output. This involves formulating realistic measures of output for each of the many cost centres which may exist in business. In a further, and very desirable refinement of this exercise, standard unit costs are set up for each cost centre so that the actual unit cost may be related from time to time to the standard. The word 'cost' is thus associated with output and, since the figures must be

collected over a period, also with time. Thus, the cost o
operating a machine may be expressed as a machine-hou
rate.

The work involved in producing unit costs for ever
operation in a business may appear overwhelming and, i
fact, such a system is likely to be developed more in th
works or centre of direct operations than in the admini
strative and sales departments. This is probably the result o
costing having originated in productive concerns but, wit
the growth of administrative functions which characterize
modern business, the logic of confining costing to the factory
is no longer apparent. Moreover the availability of compute
services removes much of the problem of processing th
data. It is, furthermore, suggested that many investigation
of departmental efficiency through the medium of unit costs
could be conducted on an *ad hoc* basis and are likely to
prove more effective than the periodic investigation o
budget variances.

The following example attempts to illustrate in figures the
points made above:

Suppose that last year the total expenses of a small business
manufacturing a standard product were recorded under its
three main departments, as follows:

	production	*sales*	*admin*	TOTAL
wages & salaries	£100,000	20,000	10,000	130,000
materials	200,000	5,000	6,000	211,000
other expenses	300,000	15,000	14,000	329,000
totals	£600,000	40,000	30,000	670,000

Assume also that in order to measure the output in each
of the three departments the following units were considered
appropriate and the outputs as shown were recorded:

Production: number of products produced   1,200,000
Sales: number of orders taken   160,000
Administration: number of employees   60

It would now be possible to calculate the unit cost in each department by dividing the output into the expenses, with the following result:

	production per unit produced	*sales* per order	*admin* per employee
wages & salaries	£0·083	0·125	167·00
materials	0·167	0·031	100·00
other expenses	0·250	0·094	233·00
totals	£0·500	0·250	500·00

The above may be considered the nucleus of a simple costing system. These unit costs could be compared with similar figures for the previous year and the trend of the results charted at, say, monthly intervals in the future. A further useful development would be to formulate standard unit costs for each department and to use those standards as a basis for comparison with the actual results month by month.

Assume that in fact the business decided to adopt the above unit costs as standards and that the expenses and output for the first month of the following year were as follows:

	production	*sales*	*admin*	TOTAL
wages & salaries	£12,000	2,000	1,000	15,000
materials	20,000	500	600	21,100
other expenses	28,000	1,300	1,400	30,700
totals	£60,000	3,800	3,000	66,800

production in units	125,000
sales orders	16,000
Admin: number of employees	70

By setting the actual unit costs of the month against the standards, the following picture emerges:

Production costs per unit produced

	standard	actual
wages & salaries	£0·083	0·096
materials	0·167	0·160
other expenses	0·250	0·224
totals	£0·500	0·480

Production costs are shown to have fallen overall, the increase in wages and salaries being offset by economies in the usage of materials and in other expenses.

Sales costs per order

	standard	actual
wages & salaries	£0·125	0·125
materials	0·031	0·031
other expenses	0·094	0·081
totals	£0·250	0·237

Sales costs correspond to standard except for a fall in other expenses, no doubt due to the fact that some of these expenses will be 'fixed' in the short term and thus unaffected by the increase in activity.

Administrative costs per employee (using $\frac{1}{12}$ of the annual standard)

	standard	actual
wages & salaries	£13·9	14·3
materials	8·3	8·6
other expenses	19·4	20·0
totals	£41·6	42·9

Administrative costs are generally higher than standard and this fact calls for investigation.

Unfortunately business, and hence costing systems, tend to be somewhat more complex than the above illustration indicates, and the absolute validity of the calculations made could be questioned on a number of grounds. Nevertheless the danger of any attempt to introduce excessive sophistication into the system may obscure the message shown by the figures. Costing, like most other accounting techniques, gives only guides for investigation and subsequent action; it does not and cannot usurp management.

What are the objectives of costing?

The costing function produces nothing other than figures and at the same time incurs considerable expense in any substantial business in the form of salaries, paper and the cost of accounting machinery. Less directly, the costing function occupies valuable space, may employ computer time, and certainly involves operational managers in lengthy consideration of cost figures. The job of the managers is to supervise the operations of engineering, buying, making and selling, and the costing system can justify its expense only if it aids these processes. The basic question is whether the business would achieve its objectives equally well without a costing system.

The answer to this question lies in first considering the desirable objectives of the costing system and then appraising the extent to which it achieves these objectives. The science of costing has developed so rapidly over the last fifty years or so, and its applications have become so complex, that its basic objectives may have become obscured. It has certainly accumulated a body of mystique which must be particularly irritating to the practical manager. The following list of objectives may be considered an over-simplification, but is at least an attempt to penetrate the mystique.

1. To assist managers in their functions of forward planning and controlling the operations for which they are responsible;
2. To assist in the determination of price and pricing policy;
3. To value work in progress and stocks as an essential element in the accounting process of profit ascertainment.

The validity of this statement of objectives is examined in the succeeding sections of this chapter and the methods of achieving the objectives form the subject matter of subsequent chapters.

Costing as an aid to forward planning

Before considering the extent to which costing can assist managers in their important function of forward planning it may be useful first to consider the question: Forward planning for what purpose? If the purpose can be defined, then the place of costing in achieving that purpose can be examined.

It appears that at a given point of time a business will have many objectives, both in the short and the long term, each of which will influence the forward planning of the management team. A common objective is growth, which may take the form of acquisitions, development geographically, obtaining a greater market share, entering into new segments of the market, extending or creating markets and launching new products. Has costing any relevance to these objectives? The answer to this question lies in the assumption that before a business embarks on a programme of development, it must consider the likely profitability of the projected enterprise. The assessment of potential profits involves an assessment of the additional expenses to be incurred. This is essentially a matter of budgeting and forecasting rather than costing, but the budgets will be more rationally formulated if they are based on the unit cost of the various operations involved in the development, or the effect of the development on the unit cost of the existing cost centres. In short the expense involved in any form of development is fundamentally a matter of multiplying the expected activity by the unit costs of each function or operation already in the business or to be created.

The objective of profit maximization in relation to forward planning is the subject of recurrent criticism, but it certainly remains a major preoccupation of the smaller business and may even be suspected of influencing operations in the larger concern. Even if the objective of a business is not the maximization of profit, the achievement of a reasonable surplus appears to be necessary for survival. The major justification of a costing system is its capacity for enabling managers to assess the relative profitability of alternative plans. These plans may embrace, for example, changes in products, in methods of production, in the use of plant, in make or buy policy and in the volume of output.

Once again, for these purposes the costing rates must be looked at afresh for they will be affected by additional expenses, savings in existing expenses and allocations of resources to the new situation. If this is true it is not simply a question, as is sometimes asserted, of dealing with alternative plans on the basis of marginal costs (a subject discussed later in somewhat greater depth). Marginal cost, that is, the additional cost of additional output, will certainly enter into the calculations but not, it is suggested, exclusively.

One of the most useful and fundamental devices for dealing with cost movements which arise from changes in operations, is to divide the expenses of the plant or workshop into their fixed or variable elements. Fixed expenses, more appropriately described as 'period costs', are those which do not change *in the short term* in accordance with changes in the activity of the business or the department of a business. The more obvious examples of fixed expenses are the rent and rates of the business premises, depreciation (based on time, not activity) and usually a substantial proportion of the administration charges. Variable expenses are those which are presumed to vary directly in relation to activity. These are clearly rough classifications, both containing a number of 'grey areas' where certain items of cost will move as a result of a great variety of factors arising in the business, or from external causes. Subject to these qualifications, it will be important for managers to know the body of costs within their responsibility which will be largely unaffected by increases or decreases in their work load, and those which are likely to move generally in harmony with changes in the volume of output.

A simple illustration of the use of this dual classification of expense is shown below.

EXAMPLE

A small jobbing engineers charges £2 an hour. It is offered an additional order at £1·4 an hour and the problem is whether this additional order shall be accepted. The present costs work out at £1·6 an hour so that on the face of the situation the additional order should be declined on the grounds that it will reduce profits. The additional order will absorb 20,000 additional hours and this requirement could be met by engaging more operatives. The relevant figures are as follows:

	present situation 100,000 hours	proposed situation 120,000 hours
VARIABLE EXPENSES	£	£
labour	80,000	96,000
consumable stores	10,000	12,000
power	2,000	2,400
other variables	5,000	6,000
	£97,000	116,400
SEMI-VARIABLE EXPENSES		
postage & stationery	5,000	5,500
telephone	1,500	1,600
clerical salaries	8,000	8,800
other semi-variables	12,500	13,700
	£27,000	29,600
FIXED EXPENSES		
rent & rates	5,000	5,000
depreciation	11,000	11,000
supervision & management	20,000	20,000
	£36,000	£36,000
Total expenses	£160,000	182,000
rate per hour	£1·60	£1·52

It is noted that the overall rate per hour would reduce
slightly if the new order were taken and this reduction is

clearly due: (a) to the semi-variable expenses not having increased in proportion to the increase in activity and; (b) to the fixed expenses having remained unaltered. The new rate is, however, still well above the rate of £1·4 an hour receivable on the additional order. Nevertheless, the new order should be accepted because it will produce additional profit for the business, as shown by the following statement:

	present situation £	proposed situation £
Income		
100,000 hours @ £2	200,000	200,000
20,000 hours @ £1·4		28,000
	£200,000	£228,000
Less: expenses	160,000	182,000
Profit	£40,000	46,000

The reason for the increased profit is that the costing rate calculated on the basis of the *additional* expenses to be incurred by the order is well below the price obtainable for the order, i.e.,

Income from additional order 20,000 hours @ £1·4	£28,000
Expenses of additional order 20,000 hours @ $\frac{£22,000}{20,000}$ = £1·1	22,000
	£6,000

The above example is intended to illustrate the danger of

using existing costing rates when appraising management's plans and of the need to consider the varying effect those plans could have on the cost structure of the business. At the same time the very simplicity of the figurework shown conceals a number of practical problems which are equally relevant to this kind of situation. Some of the further questions which need to be answered are set out below.

1. If the business is at present working to capacity, then the additional order could cause an increase in the facilities represented by the so-called fixed costs, e.g., in more space, plant and supervision.
2. If the business is not working to capacity, then the implication is that the fixed facilities (and possibly some of the semi-variable costs) are not being used to the full on existing work. Thus the real rate per hour on existing work is below the £1·60 shown. It also follows that part of the cost of the idle facilities is applicable to the new order. If, and only if, those facilities could be used remuneratively in another direction, then the new order may in fact be unprofitable.
3. The new order may also be unprofitable if the low price at which it is taken causes a reduction in the price obtainable on existing orders.

The use of costing in connection with pricing problems is further discussed in the next section.

Cost and the determination of price

It has been suggested above that profit-making is fundamentally a question of finding the best combination of price, volume and costs. If this statement has any substance, then it means that in a given situation there should, in theory, be one 'right price' at which to place a product or service on the market. This is the price which, in conjunction with a certain level of turnover and costs will produce the greatest profit in a given period.

Admittedly, in particular circumstances, pricing policy may well have objectives other than that of the maximization of profit, especially short-term profit. Such other objectives may take the form of increasing the market share, keeping competitors out of a new market, maintaining customer goodwill and so forth. Even with a purely profit objective the business may be satisfied with a reasonable return on capital and will not attempt to maximize that return.

Although other objectives than profit maximization may dictate pricing policy, there would still be merit in first establishing the price at which profit is greatest, as this price would act as a datum line from which to measure off the adjustments required by marketing tactics or business policy. This is another way of saying that it is entirely up to management how they choose to apply the profit potential of a project; they may, indeed, use part of such potential profit to reduce price. They may be forced to do so by government edict.

Perhaps because business covers so wide a field, it is difficult to find in the literature on the subject any universal rules to aid in deciding the right price for a product or service. The economist's analysis of the effect of price on demand, or vice versa, appears too abstract for practical application, especially when on occasions the businessman sees that a low price will deter customers and a high price may encourage them. The subject is further complicated by the diversity of policies and intentions, and the marketing tactics which may influence the pricing decision. The immediate question is the extent to which costs can or should influence that decision.

Ostensibly the problem can be divided into two parts: (a) the desirability of changing the price of existing products, and (b) the pricing of new products. In both cases a major factor, and often the decisive factor, will be the influence of the market in the sense of both the willingness and the ability of various groups of customers to pay a particular price. The influence of the market is noticeably strongest where strong competition exists, but even in those circumstances cost is likely to have a long-term influence because when the market price falls to a point which no longer justifies production, the shortage of supplies will tend to force up the price again. Cost tends in practice to have the greatest influence in the pricing of new products, particularly where there is little competition at the point of launching the product. In such circumstances, however, the idea that a theoretically 'right price' can be arrived at by calculation, may be qualified by marketing tactics. Thus it may be decided that the best policy is to 'skim' the market by charging a high price until the advent of competition enforces a reduction; or the contrary policy of charging the lowest possible price may be adopted to deter competition as long as possible. In a great deal of contract work, especially with government contracts, price is essentially a function of cost, but the market will have a long-term effect.

The foregoing very brief review is intended merely to indicate the complexities of the subject. The conclusion is that the major factors influencing price are: policy, marketing tactics, competition, demand and cost. These factors affect the situation with varying emphases according to the nature of the business, the product and the long- or short-term aspects. So far as cost is concerned, the important consideration is to ensure that cost is properly assessed for the purpose.

It has been suggested in the preceding section that costs are essentially dependent (amongst other factors) on volume of output. Changes in volume will have different effects on variable, semi-variable and period or fixed costs. Where the short term only is in question the relevant costs will be the marginal costs, or the additional outgoings incurred by additional output. In the long term, consideration must be given to the use of existing facilities which could be applied to other remunerative purposes. In neither case is the cost derived from the routine costing system, which is basically constructed to value work in progress, the relevant cost.

In the present context the objective of pricing policy must be to make at least the minimum profit which will satisfy those who have invested in the concern. Essentially, it is suggested, this means a reasonably long-term view of profit because normally a well-founded business will be able to weather a temporary reduction in profitability. Profit is not necessarily maximized by charging the highest price the market will bear for the reason that, if that market is at all elastic, a high price may reduce turnover below an economic level. Conversely, the lower limit to which price can be reduced in the long term to achieve higher turnover is the relevant cost. Thus there is almost always a price range within which the pricing decision can be made. The secret lies in finding the balance between price, turnover and total expenses which will produce the optimum profit.

Using the simplest of figures to illustrate the points made above, assume that last year's sales of a domestic product gave the following result:

price per unit	£5
units sold	150,000
sales value	£750,000
Less: variable costs at £3 a unit	450,000
Contribution towards fixed costs and profit	£300,000
fixed costs	250,000
Profit	£50,000

In seeking ways of increasing the profit the management estimate that: (a) if the price were reduced to £4 they would be able to sell 200,000 units; but (b) if the price were increased to £5·50 a unit, the sales would fall to 130,000 units in a year. For the sake of this illustration the rather rash assumptions are made that fixed costs will remain at £250,000, that the *rate* of variable costs per unit will be unaltered, and that the management is able to predict the

nfluence of price on volume, i.e., the elasticity of demand.
Given these assumptions the alternatives may be expressed
s follows:

1. *Reduce price to £4*

sales, units	200,000
sales, value	£800,000
Less: variable costs @ £3	600,000
contribution	£200,000
Less: fixed costs	250,000
Loss	£50,000

2. *Increase price to £5·50*

sales, units	130,000
sales, value	£715,000
Less: variable costs @ £3	390,000
contribution	£325,000
Less: fixed costs	250,000
Profit	£75,000

Thus, in this illustration profitability could be improved
by increasing the price, but the opposite *might* have been the
case. Nor does the example indicate that a further increase
in price will yield greater profits, because turnover might
thereby be reduced disproportionately and overall profits
might then fall. It is just conceivable that a more substantial
reduction in price would create so great a rise in turnover as
to yield the best solution. Furthermore, the simple arithmetical solution shown above ignores many of the realities

of business, such as the fact that in many cases differential prices apply to various segments of the market, e.g., the use of discounts for customer classes; the possibility that increased turnover will cause a rise in fixed costs, if only in the increased usage of plant and storage space; the probability that the rate of variable costs will fall with higher output because of the effect of the economies of long runs.

Most of the complexities of this kind of assessment can be expressed in the form of a simple mathematical model but it needs to be appreciated that such a model is only as accurate as the estimates with which it is constructed. It is however, a reasonable conclusion that costs, properly used can give some real guidance in the determination of price but they will by no means be decisive.

The valuation of stocks and work in progress

Profit as shown in business accounts is determined by periodically revaluing the assets and the liabilities of a business. The surprising thing is that not every businessman appreciates the fundamentally simple process by which the profit of his business is ascertained. To the accountant profit is nothing more sophisticated than the amount by which the net assets of a business have increased compared with the position at the previous accounting period. The function of the profit and loss account and subsidiary statements is to list the categories of income which have added value to the business, and the categories of expenditure which represent losses of value. The real problems which arise in arriving at a true and fair view of profit are problems of valuation. The value of anything varies widely according to the purpose of the valuation, the point of view of the valuer, the circumstances existing at the time of valuation, and innumerable other factors; it is common experience that two people will value the same thing at perhaps widely different prices.

Thus, in calculating asset values which will appear in the balance sheet, and will affect the figure of profit, the accountant is forced to apply a number of sometimes quite flexible conventions for the purpose of producing a figure of profit which is consistent, that is to say, comparable from year to year. The established accounting conventions cannot conceivably cover every circumstance and thus, in addition, the process of valuing assets and ascertaining profit necessarily involves also a substantial exercise of judgement, even opinion. It is hardly surprising that from time to time the accountant's conventions are attacked as being out of date and inappropriate to the current circumstances of business.

It is important for the businessman to understand the conventions which apply to the valuation of stocks for two reasons: the first is that stocks can form a very large proportion of the assets of a business, and the second is that the traditional conventions applicable to the valuation of stocks represent one of the targets of criticisms of accounting methods. In the present context it is convenient to consider stocks under the following three main headings: (a) raw materials, including bought-out components for further processing; (b) work in progress; and (c) finished goods ready for sale. The convention generally applied in valuing these assets at the end of a period of account is simple enough: it is that they shall be valued at cost unless their net realizable value is below cost, when the latter basis will apply.

The convention is simple enough to understand but in practice a number of complexities arise in interpreting the terms 'cost' and 'net realizable value'. The calculation of 'cost' is the outcome of an accounting, or more strictly, costing process, which will be outlined below. 'Net realizable value' is synonymous with market value for finished goods or stock for sale; and for work in progress it normally means the saleable value of the finished product less the further costs required to complete the processes involved. The concept of net realizable value is certainly not without its difficulties of interpretation in exceptional cases but this particular matter is somewhat outside the scope of this book. The relevant question is the old one: What is cost?

In the case of a comparatively simple business, such as retail shop, the stock consists solely of goods for sale. such a case the valuation of the stock will take the form an annual or more frequent stocktaking which involv applying to each item its 'cost', i.e., the price paid for it.

Even this tedious but fairly routine exercise is not witho its problems, such as where it is necessary to reduce the co price of the goods where they have deteriorated, are difficu to sell or are slow moving. It will be observed that the effe of the cost basis of valuation is to defer recording profit the goods until they are actually sold, and this princip applies to all businesses; although it is not without its critic A further problem will arise where various items of the san class of goods have been bought at different prices. There a at least eight different methods of arriving at cost in suc cases and some writers have listed many more. The mech anics and effects of applying each of these methods will t examined later.

The essence of a costing system in a manufacturir business is that it operates on the assumption that values (terms of cost) are added to raw material in the workshop and the finished article leaves the workshops for the finishe goods store valued at the cost of the raw material and th bought-out components plus the values added in the work shop of workmen's time, machine time and other overhead The resulting total is termed 'the cost' of the final produc and this is the figure which will be set off against the sale proceeds when the product is sold, and thus show the prof obtained on that article. The precise method by which pa of a man's wages is applied to a job, the calculation c machine-hour rates and other overhead rates, necessaril involve assumptions and conventions; the final figure o 'cost' is not an absolute fact or a precise measure in th sense that the weight of the output can be measured in ton: The costing principles, conventions and methods will nor mally be worked out logically and with judgement for th purposes for which they are intended. In the present contex the purposes are to produce a valuation which will give t

rofit consistency, comparability with past periods, and a
rudent view. A system at least replaces guesswork. Some-
mes the system is faulty, as the many businesses which have
crashed' with overvalued stock bear witness.

The conclusion to this chapter can only be a reiteration
f what was said at the beginning: that a cost is only valid
vhen applied to the purpose for which it was intended. In
ther words it is only relevant costs which are useful to
nanagement: neither historical nor standard costs, marginal
or replacement costs, nor even opportunity costs, have any
laims as panaceas unless they are relevant to the purpose
equired. The applications of these concepts of cost will be
liscussed in the next chapter.

2 Elements of Cost

*The basic elements; Direct labour costing; Overtime;
Direct materials: nature; procedure for collecting the
costs; pricing material issues*

The basic elements

Traditionally the elements of cost are labour, materials an
other expenses (or 'overheads'). In this sense the wor
'labour' is usually understood to mean the wages paid t
people working on the product or service for sale, in othe
words, direct wages. Likewise 'materials' refers to direc
materials, that is to say, the materials incorporated in th
product. 'Other expenses' is clearly an omnibus term whic
covers all the innumerable expenses of business which ar
not direct wages or direct materials. This very primitive sub
division of cost probably dates from the times when th
science of costing was in its infancy and was concentrate
on the costs incurred in the workshop or other direct centr
of operations. Clearly the complexity of a modern busines
demands an analysis of cost which, if it is to be meaningfu
must be far more detailed.

Nevertheless, the costing of labour and materials sti
constitutes the essential basis of a costing system in man
present-day organizations, especially where these costs forr
a large proportion of the total expense of the business. Th
importance of sound labour costing is also emphasized b
the disproportionate rise in wages during recent years, com
pared with other elements of cost. In 1971 Imperial Chemica

dustries Limited reported a rise of £21m in wages and
laries although the numbers employed had fallen by 5,000.
factor which is, however, tending to reduce the importance
labour costing in industry is increasing automation of
ocesses and eventually, it is said, whole plants, and the
creasing effectiveness of labour-saving systems.

There seems to be no reason to suppose that material costs
ill diminish in amount, particularly where that cost was
timately created by labour; and if this is so material is
kely to remain an important element of cost. However, in
usinesses providing a service, those largely dependent on
pital equipment, or where there is a need for a strong
arketing and distribution function, the *proportion* of
aterial cost to total cost may be small.

The growth in business functions only indirectly associ-
ed with the direct operations of producing the goods or
rvices for sale is tending to lessen the importance of the
roduction cost. This is particularly true where, as mentioned
ove, survival in a highly competitive market is dependent
a large extent on publicity, sales, service and highly
eveloped planning, management information and con-
olling functions. The continued development of com-
uterized data-processing and production control may be
ssening direct production costs but is at the same time
creasing indirect or 'overhead' expenses.

Another factor which is reducing the emphasis on labour
nd material costing, and indeed on all kinds of current
roduction costs is the expenditure required in plant, sys-
ms, training and other forms of investment. Thus a sub-
antial element of the costs of producing and selling a
roduct consists of deferred charges, by which is meant
xpenses incurred and paid for but appropriate to the income
f later years. When such costs are in fact carried forward
o be set off against the future sales which they are assumed
o generate, they become uncontrollable, because the money
as been spent. If they are charged against current sales,
hen they are not properly related to such sales. Research
nd development is a typical example of such deferred

charges, but in strictness plant costs are also of this natu because they are deferred by the depreciation device.

Thus it seems that a more detailed analysis of costs th; the simple division into labour, materials and overheads necessary in the modern age; and some more useful a; proaches will be considered later. Meanwhile it is necessa; to point out that many very large industrial concerns a; content to base their costing systems on direct labo; and direct material, applying to direct labour costs ; overhead rate which is designed to 'recover' (as the sayi; goes) the overheads of the concern. 'Recovering' ove heads in this sense simply means grossing up the labo; and materials costs by a percentage. Not a penny is ; fact 'recovered' until the eventual product is sold ar paid for.

Whilst the validity of the simple method of costing ou lined in the previous paragraph may be questioned, th widespread use of such a system justifies some examinatio of the methods used and of the problems involved.

Direct labour costing

Subject to various differences between undertakings as t the precise mechanics employed, direct labour costing mear recording the time taken by operatives in a works o processes, works orders, batches, or whatever unit is selecte for costing, and applying to that time an hourly rate corre ponding to the rate payable to the employee concernec Because in some factories an enormous number of hourl rates are in effect, it is usually considered sufficiently accura; to grade the operatives under a limited number of categorie and to calculate for each of these categories an averag hourly rate. In simple applications the time taken on jobs ; recorded manually by the operatives concerned on tim sheets or similar documents. In more sophisticated system the time of starting and ending on a job is recorded, often b shop clerks, by means of time recording machines, thu giving an impressive but often spurious appearance c

ccuracy to the record. By the same means bookings are
ade of idle time under such headings as: waiting for work,
ttending sick bay, attending meetings, waiting for materials
nd other categories of idle time; assuming they are accurate,
ese are the statistics of real use to shop-floor management
1 controlling efficiency.

At daily or, more usually, weekly intervals the times
ooked by each man against the several jobs in progress are
ultiplied in the cost office by the appropriate hourly rates,
nd the product of this exercise is collated under the job
umbers, thus arriving at the labour cost of each job in the
eriod. With a computerized or mechanized system the time
ookings may be entered on to punched cards or tape and
he calculations and collations made by the computer or
ther mechanical device. The computer enables enormous
mounts of detailed calculations and records to be processed
vith great speed and arithmetical accuracy. As a result of
he intricate mechanical and electronic operations involved,
nuch of which may be imperfectly understood by shop-floor
nanagement, the eventual tabulation takes on an even
greater appearance of the ultimate truth, but the basic
nformation fed into the system and the machine may be
uspect.

The question as to whether or not the labour costs are
uspect will depend largely on two factors: (a) the integrity
vith which the time recordings have been made; and (b) the
nature of the information which the controlling managers
need to know. Many labour costing systems were designed
o meet the requirements of many years ago, and unfortunately once a system has been installed and programmed on
a computer a major operation is often necessary before the
ystem can be altered to meet current managerial needs. The
levelopment of electronic data-processing systems means in
many cases that subordinate managers, who are directly in
charge of the workpeople, have no say in the nature of the
nformation they receive. In some cases they may be under
a complete misapprehension as to the objectives of the
nformation which is produced. More often, they suspect

that it is inapplicable to their requirements and ignore i creating their own sub-systems.

Thus, before a labour costing system is installed it important that its objectives should be clearly stated. If, take an extreme case to illustrate the argument, the objecti of labour costing is to record the highest possible labo costs against each job, stopping short, of course, of delibe ate falsity, then the key is to reduce idle time bookings the minimum. Waiting for material might, in such a situatio be treated as part of the cost of doing a job. The fact that particular worker is slow, whether because of lack of skill lack of inclination, will make his times longer than norm and, of course, add to the values costed to the jobs h undertakes and, incidentally, add to the value of work progress. This apparently extreme illustration is not u known in connection with jobs remunerated on an actu cost basis. Such an approach to labour costing may well justified on the grounds that it produces the highest price f the eventual product, but it is clearly useless for the purpos of planning and controlling performance. It will inevitabl lead to an interesting competitive spirit between the variou workshops of the plant, to determine which shop can ama the greatest cost and the most complete 'recovery' of ove heads applied to labour costs.

It is sometimes argued that a system of costing so-calle 'actual' labour costs on the lines indicated above enable controlling management to see where costs are high. Th objection to this argument is that the determination as t whether costs are high depends on a comparison, and wit 'actual' costing the comparison can only be with past cost But past costs may also have been high due to inefficienc and whilst a reduction will show improvement it will no necessarily show efficiency. Furthermore, the situation whe the past costs were recorded may well be substantiall different from the current situation, for even with standar dized methods of production the comparison may becom falsified by changes in wage rate, new methods, improve materials and more efficient machinery.

The solution to the problems of labour costing for control rposes lies, it is suggested, in the establishment of realistic ndard times and rates representing those applicable to icient working, and to record by jobs or other units only e standard costs. Many companies record standards side side with actual costs, thus duplicating the clerical work volved, but a case will be submitted later for avoiding this plication of effort and at the same time retaining all the vantages of control through standard costing.

In connection with this subject, modern developments row doubt on the validity of the assumption, implicit in ditional labour costing, that a man's weekly wage can be alistically apportioned to the several jobs he works on ring the week. The apparent assumption implicit in bour costing is that if, for example, a man works four urs on a job and his hourly rate is calculated at 50p per ur, therefore the job has cost the organization £2·00 in bour. Modern conditions of employment as, for instance, idenced by such legislation as the Contracts of Employ- nt Act and the Redundancy Pay Act, suggest that employ- s are paid weekly or monthly amounts in consideration of eir *availability* to do work in the period, not because they ve performed certain specific jobs. Thus the wage bill of a mpany is as much a time cost (i.e., variable with time, not th jobs) as is the electricity bill. Each of those items of pense can certainly be terminated, but in each case with a nalty.

vertime

he basic problem with regard to the costing of overtime, with incentive schemes, is the question whether the remium paid for the overtime or, in the case of incentive hemes, the additional output, should be treated as a direct large against the job or added to factory overheads. onsider first the general problem in relation to overtime orking.

Assume that an operative is paid at the basic rate of 50p

an hour and that he takes two hours to complete a particul
task. If he works beyond normal times on the job duri
weekdays, assume he is paid time + 1/5th for the wor
Assume for the sake of this example that no further incenti
scheme is in operation. The different amounts payable to t
operative will be:

For working in normal times: 2 hours @ £0·50 = £1·
For working in overtime: 2·4 hours @ £0·50 = £1·

In this case the premium paid for the overtime working
£0·20 and the question is whether this amount shall
charged to the job or added to overheads, to be eventual
applied to all jobs carried out during the period by means
an overhead rate.

The normal method of treating the premium is to char
it to overheads so that the job is charged with labour cos
at the basic wage rate whether the work is actually done
normal time or in overtime. The justification for such trea
ment is that the need for overtime working is an incident
production planning, i.e., a management charge, and it
unreasonable to assume that the job which happened to
scheduled for completion by overtime working was the o
which should bear the extra cost. It may well be, moreove
that the need for working overtime on a particular job aro
because another job took longer to complete in normal wor
ing times than was expected.

Frequently an exception to this general rule is mad
where the customer requires urgent delivery of an order an
is prepared to pay for the overtime premium so necessitate
To the present writer the making of an exception to a logic
rule for the reasons stated seems to be a confusion betwee
costing and pricing; this is not an infrequent malaise
industry which has traditions based on a less competitiv
age. It may well be that the customer is prepared to r
imburse the manufacturer for the overtime premium b
this fact does not justify a departure from the principle

osting overtime to overheads, assuming that principle was ight in the first place.

The real objection to operating the principles of costing vertime premium to overheads lies in the fact that in many ndustries a proportion of overtime working has become the ormal rather than the exception. A frequent question put o employment officers when operatives (and sometimes lerical staff) apply for jobs is: What overtime can be xpected? It may be unjust to suggest that an element in the ressure for a shorter working week is the expectation that his would bring not less working hours but more overtime ay. Certainly most employees are interested in their 'take-ome pay' and it is not unknown for sufficient overtime to e organized so that an employee will obtain the same take-ome pay which he could expect from another employer ompeting for his services. A business may ensure that in ormal conditions of trade a reasonable amount of overtime as to be worked; and this system gives them flexibility to educe costs by limiting overtime during slack periods of rade.

The practical issues outlined in the preceding paragraph uggest that, where a proportion of overtime working has ecome normal, the costing of the overtime premium to verheads is likely to result in the labour element of job osts being somewhat less than actual. It is not suggested hat the jobs actually carried out in the overtime periods hould bear the overtime premium but that the hourly rates hould be adjusted to cover normal overtime premium ayments.

In this connection it is relevant to point out that, in any vent, the cost of labour applied directly to saleable products s not by any means limited to the wages or salary paid. So alled 'fringe benefits', in the form of national insurance, uperannuation, etc, materially add to the cost of employing eople and may be around 7% of pay or more. Standard ourly rates could well embrace these employee charges as vell as customary overtime premiums.

Direct materials

THE NATURE OF DIRECT MATERIAL COSTS

Direct material costs may be defined as the material costs which can be applied to units of output (e.g., operations, jobs, batches, contracts, products, etc) with reasonable precision, convenience and economy.

There is a common belief that, of all the elements of cost, direct materials must be closest to absolute fact, and the qualifications inherent in the above definition may cause some surprise. Nevertheless, the discussion which follows in this section will suggest that even with direct material costs there are wide variations in permissible treatment. For example, the need to qualify the word 'precision' by the word 'reasonable' in the definition suggested above will become apparent when, later in this section, the various methods of valuing material issued to production are examined. The qualifications of 'convenience' and 'economy' are necessary, for the difficulty and cost of ascertaining the value of some materials actually incorporated in the product become prohibitive. Generally, paint and small items of hardware, such as nuts, bolts, screws and rivets, fall into this category.

The fact that the cost of raw material in a product cannot be stated with absolute accuracy does not reduce the importance of a scientific and logically thought-out material costing system. It is common knowledge that material constitutes a high proportion of total production cost in many industries. Furthermore, material may be said to represent the bedrock of costing in a manufacturing business, for the operations of such a business may be looked upon as a process of adding values, in the form of labour, machine time and other services, to the material which enters the factory. This is a viewpoint of manufacture which has even been belatedly recognized in the advent of Value Added Tax to the United Kingdom. Unlike the Value Added Tax, however, a costing system does not normally accept that value is added by the general company administrative

ervices nor by the operation of selling the product, however
ssential those services may be. The values shown to be
dded in the normal manufacturing costing system are those
onfined to the productive effort.

DDING VALUES IN THE STOCK ACCOUNTS

The process of adding values to raw material in a manu-
acturing business is reflected in the stock accounts, which
asically comprise raw material stock, work in progress and
nished goods, and is illustrated in the following example.
n this example stages have been introduced in an attempt to
larify the exposition.

	quantity	price £	value £
Stage 1			
,000 units of a certain raw material, priced at £1 a unit, are delivered and entered in the Raw Material Stores Account. The various categories of material are analysed by material numbers in the costing records	1,000	1·00	1,000
Stage 2			
800 of the units of material are drawn from stores by the workshop for the job and are entered in Work in Progress Account	800	1·00	800
Leaving in Raw Material Stores	200	£1·00	£200

	quantity	price	value
		£	£

Stage 3

To the value of raw material in work in progress of	800	1·00	800

there are added bought-out components	500	0·50	250

direct labour applied to the fabrication of the material	200 hrs	£0·75	150
overheads at £0·75 an hour			150

Giving a total in work in progress of (This total is analysed in the Cost Ledger or other form of record by job numbers.)			£1,350

Stage 4

As the work is completed the finished products are transferred from the workshop to the finished goods store at an estimated value. Assume that in a given period 200 complete products are manufactured and the estimated cost is £2·50 each	200	2·50	500

Leaving in Work in Progress Account a value of			£850

Stage 5

From the value of finished goods stock of	200	2·50	500
One-half (say) are sold and delivered to customers, the production cost of the goods sold being	100	2·50	250
Leaving in Finished Goods Stock Account	100	£2·50	£250

If it is assumed that each finished product incurred the cost of two units of material (units might be a measure of length or weight), then it can be said that the finished product contains values added to the raw material of £0·50 each.

The system of accounting which is implicit in the foregoing necessarily generalized outline of the procedure, involves integrating the costing system into the so-called 'financial' accounting system. In other words, the records of unit costs, whether of material or jobs in the workshop break down into the required units the total expenses and values shown in the main account, particularly the stock accounts. Much of the information for the main accounts is derived from the costing records, and the whole represents one system, not two.

The reader experienced in these matters will recognize the possibility of many anomalies in the basic system outlined above. In particular, the stock values may be inflated by inefficiency due to high prices of material, excess usage, unnecessarily long labour times and high overhead rates. The value of the finished goods stock will depend on the estimated cost at which it is transferred from work in progress, and the same factor will directly affect the gross profit. The remedy for such anomalies is discussed under the chapter on Standard Costing where the same basic information is used.

THE PROCEDURE FOR COLLECTING THE COSTS

The foregoing example suggests that in a manufacturin business direct materials pass through five more or le distinct stages in the manufacturing process. These stage denote the points at which the material passes in and out c the various locations where it is temporarily stored; th progress being indicated by the following chart:

The Business

Supplier   raw material   work in   finished goods   custo
         stores   progress   stores   mer

Obviously in a large and complex operation a number c sub-stores and sub-locations will need to be established, an this is particularly so in a factory where the material passe through a number of processes.

Sub stores will in effect contain the tangible result of eac process during the manufacturing operation, and the wor will accumulate further value as it proceeds from one oper ation to another. The whole may then form a network which for control purposes, may be amenable to critical patl analysis. In the manufacture of complex machinery o instrumentation it will often be desirable for complete components to be removed from the shop floor and place in separate stores pending demands from the next process or for service parts. When components are placed in sub stores it is desirable that the appropriate stores account record the make-up of their value in terms of labour material, bought-out parts and overheads, so that the cos of the final assembly is also recorded under these elements

    The need to maintain records analysed by the cost ele ments for each sub store, is to aid in the control of th various expenses which are incurred in making a componen or carrying out a process. The total values in each store a any one time will be recorded in the general 'financial accounting system and the costs of each item or quantity passing in and out of that store will be derived from the

osting system. Likewise the costing system will record the
osts of each job or operation which is built into the cost of
component or process.

In order that the necessary clerical, analysing and collating
xercises shall be carried out by the costing function, it is
ssential that accurate information as to added values and
novements of the resulting material are transmitted to that
unction from the workshops. As a result a large volume of
aperwork passes from the operating departments to the
osting department and, because of occasional human errors,
corresponding effort is required in checking the validity of
he information. A good system and good form design will
ninimize the paperwork and reduce the need for checking
ut the services of an internal audit department (particu-
arly applied to stock audit) can promote both efficiency and
ccuracy in paperwork. Computerized data-processing can
educe much of the human effort involved and, although it
nay substitute punched tape or punched cards for hand-
vritten forms, some form of input record for the information
vill be essential.

The basic documents are the following:

. *Goods Received Note.* Used as a basis for entries into the
   Raw Material Stores Account and for the costing analysis
   of that account by classifications of material.
2. *Requisition.* Used to withdraw material from stores for
   processing in the workshop. Credit requisitions are used
   for material returned to stores. Requisitions are valued
   and analysed by material classifications (for stores
   records) and by jobs (for work in progress job costs).
3. *Delivery Note for Finished Stock.* This form, when valued
   at the assessed cost of the finished product, is the basis of
   the withdrawal of value from the Work in Progress
   Account and the individual job totals, and the addition
   to Finished Goods Account, which will, in turn, be
   analysed by product groups, contracts, etc.
4. *Delivery Note to Customer.* This document, which may be

prepared by the same operation as the invoice is prepared
is valued at the assessed cost of the product sold, and i
used to record the withdrawal of value from the Finishe
Stock Account and the charge to the Trading Account o
the cost of the goods sold.

THE PROBLEM OF PRICING MATERIAL ISSUES

A pricing or valuation exercise is involved for each move
ment of material from one location to another. Superficiall
it would appear that no special accounting problems aris
in valuing the withdrawal from stores of, say, copper ba
bought for £420 a ton. Problems do in fact arise because, a
a matter of common experience, purchases are made a
different prices, and at a given point of time the stock con
sists of varying quantities of material bought at variou
prices. But the problem is not really one of deciding whic
quantity purchased shall be used first but of settling
material pricing policy. The policy chosen will affect no
only the unit costs for control purposes, but also the valu
ation of stocks and work in progress, the figure of capita
employed and the trend of profits as shown in the accounts

The policy to be used for pricing material issues is mor
of a management problem than an accounting problem. Th
fundamental question is whether the issues shall be value
at some variant of historical cost, at standard cost or a
replacement cost. This is a matter of policy which, once it i
established, must apply not only to material but also to th
other elements of cost, if the accounting is to have th
desirable quality of consistency. It would be illogical if i
were decided that, for example, material costs should be o
a replacement basis whereas historical cost should be use
for depreciation.

Once the costing policy has been decided it is then neces
sary to choose the costing convention for the implementatio
of that policy; by which is meant, in the case of historica
costing, whether to use the first in first out, average price, o
some other convention. For this purpose the circumstance
of the business are likely to be relevant. These circumstance

would undoubtedly include the resources available for coping with the clerical effort and the capacity of the managers for comprehending the effects of the method chosen. Each convention will produce a different figure of cost. This is not to say as a generalization that any particular convention, currently accepted, is wrong, for cost is itself a convention of which the implications need understanding. The principal methods used are examined below.

1. *Actual Cost*

This means that materials drawn from stores are valued (i.e., charged to work in progress) at the price at which they were purchased. The use of such a system should be confined to identifiable purchases to be used on specific jobs, such as when specially constructed equipment is acquired for a specific customer's order. In other words the application is to bought-out parts or components which are not uniform. If an attempt was made to cost standard material at actual cost, then the costing would depend on the convenience or the whim of the storekeeper; even if it were physically possible.

2. *First in, first out*

The assumption implicit in this method is that the earliest purchases should be used up first in satisfying the requirements of the works. This is a costing convention and the actual order in which the material is applied is quite irrelevant. In the case of material subject to deterioration – and there are few materials without this characteristic – good stores management would in any case probably ensure that the oldest materials were used first, and it is possible that this physical requirement was the origin of the procedure. Otherwise there seems to be no particular logic in assuming that the oldest material is used first for pricing requisitions, except, perhaps, that such a system has the merit of simplicity.

The following examples indicate the effect of the system in operation, the first being a situation when prices are rising, and the second is the less frequent situation when prices of the material concerned are falling.

week no.	additions			withdrawals			balance in stock	
	price	quantity	£	price	quantity	£	quantity	£
(a) First in First Out – Prices Rising								
10	£400	10	£4,000				10	4,000
12	420	6	2,520				16	6,520
14				£400	8	3,200	8	3,320
16				400	2 ⎫ 6	800	6	2,520
				420	4 ⎭	1,680	2	840
18	440	5	2,200				7	3,040
						£5,680		
(b) First in First Out – Prices Falling								
10	£400	10	4,000				10	4,000
12	380	6	2,280				16	6,280
14				£400	8	3,200	8	3,080
16				400	2 ⎫ 6	800	6	2,280
				380	4 ⎭	1,520	2	760
18	360	5	1,800				7	2,560
						£5,520		

3. *Average cost*

This convention means that the value of each successive issue is calculated by dividing the total value in stock by the quantity in stock. Compared with the first in first out method average cost brings the costing of issues closer to current costs. If prices are rising, the average cost method tends to show a lower stock value than the first in first out system, and a higher stock value if prices are falling.

week no.	additions price	quantity	£	withdrawals price	quantity	£	balance in stock quantity	£	average value
(a) Average Cost – Prices Rising									
10	£400	10	4,000				10	4,000	400
12	420	6	2,520				16	6,520	408
14				£408	8	3,264	8	3,256	407
16				407	6	2,442	2	814	407
18	440	5	2,200				7	3,014	431
						£5,706			
(b) Average Cost – Prices Falling									
10	£400	10	4,000				10	4,000	£400
12	380	6	2,280				16	6,280	393
14				£393	8	3,144	8	3,136	392
16				392	6	2,352	2	784	392
18	360	5	1,800				7	2,584	369
						£5,496			

4. Last in first out

This means that each withdrawal from stores is valued at the price of the most recent purchase, but if the quantity of most recent purchase is not large enough to cover the withdrawal, then the balance is valued at the price of the next preceding purchase, and so on. The presumed theoretical justification of this convention is that it brings current material costs nearer to current money values. The method is thus related to the much discussed but rarely operated philosophy of accounting which prescribes that accounts must reflect the current purchasing power of money. This philosophy is associated – perhaps confused – with the replacement theory of accounting which is examined in Chapter 4, 'Concepts of Cost' and Chapter 8, 'Replacement Costing'.

The last-in, first-out system of pricing material issues has apparently been used by few companies and those are largely located in America. It was undoubtedly introduced as a consequence of continually rising prices but has not been accepted by the taxation authorities in the UK. The latter factor complicates the issue but is hardly a decisive argument against the validity of the system. What may be considered a more convincing test of the theory is whether it is valid in all circumstances; thus if it is valid when prices are rising it should be equally valid when prices are falling. As shown by the example below, however, the effects of pricing on a last-in first-out basis, when prices are falling, are hardly likely to commend the system to practical businessmen.

The last-in, first-out system will produce material costs closer to current values and replacement values when stock is being continuously replaced; but if stock is not being replaced, such as occurs near the end of a product line, then withdrawals will have to be priced retrogressively at the price of the earlier purchases. In these circumstances the later withdrawals would be priced well below current values, assuming rising prices. This technical defect in the system can be overcome by making an arbitrary adjustment to the values shown against the older purchases, the corresponding entry in the books being to a reserve account.

Even where purchases were keeping pace with withdrawals, it would not necessarily be true to say that the price of the last purchase represented current prices because of the inevitable delay which occurs between ordering and delivery of material. However, by a small adaptation of the procedure, it would not be unduly difficult to price withdrawals from stock at the price of the last order, or even at the price being currently quoted by suppliers. Accounting procedures should be adaptable to the information requirements of the business, not the reverse. However, questions of the economy and the simplicity of administrative procedures are important in business, and once values are arbitrarily introduced into accounting systems complications ensue. Any attempt to value issues at current prices when those prices are rising has the mechanical effect of producing progressively lower stock values, unless those values are, in turn, arbitrarily adjusted.

Another complication, which cannot be ignored in the consideration of the last-in, first-out method, is that it is doubtful if in the UK it would be acceptable for the published accounts of companies, which need to be audited. Audit practice has considerable flexibility provided the accounts show a true and fair view of the results in accordance with generally accepted accounting practice, but these conditions may not obtain where a rigid adherence to the last-in first-out system is enforced. The need for an audit does not, of course, prevent the management of a company from instituting the kind of information service it requires but, if that service produces anomalies in accounting, adjustments may be required for the published accounts.

week no.	additions price	quantity	£	withdrawals price	quantity	£	balance quantity	£
(a) Last in First Out – Prices Rising								
10	£400	10	4,000				10	4,000
12	420	6	2,520				16	6,520
14				£420	6	2,520	10	4,000
				400	2	800	8	3,200
16				400	6	2,400	2	800
18	440	5	2,200				7	3,000
						£5,720		
(b) Last in First Out – Prices falling								
10	£400	10	4,000				10	4,000
12	380	6	2,280				16	6,280
14				380	6	2,280	10	4,000
				400	2	800	8	3,200
16				400	6	2,400	2	800
18	360	5	1,800				7	2,600
						£5,480		

What conclusions can be drawn from the preceding brief examination of the above somewhat esoteric accounting device for valuing material issues? The following are suggested for consideration:

1. Where stock levels are being regularly replaced the system will bring material costs nearer to current costs, but they will not necessarily be identical with current costs. This feature of the system may be considered an advantage where costs influence prices and are used as a basis for forward planning.
2. If the objective of the system is to produce costs in terms of current money values, then the same approach should be used with other elements of cost, so that the figures produced shall have consistency and comparability. With this objective in mind, the last-in, first-out pricing system would not produce the most accurate results.
3. Where withdrawals of stock are not fully replaced, the system, without arbitrary adjustment would tend to produce irrational values of stock held and irrational variations in the price of issues.
4. The final conclusion suggested is that the system is one which may be justified by expediency but hardly on the grounds of principle. On the grounds of expediency the system could be used to justify price increases, where the general price level was rising rapidly; and in a similar inflationary situation it would help to reduce the amount of distributable profit, thus strengthening the capital. It would, however seem extraordinary if these ends could only be achieved by operating a particular system of pricing material issues for costing purposes.

5. *Replacement cost*

Under this system, the whole stock, and hence the issues to the workshops are valued at the cost of replacing the stock. The replacement cost, in a sophisticated system, is not limited to the price to be paid to a supplier, but may include additions for stocking costs, covering such stock-room expenses as the cost of space, clerical effort and interest on the capital invested in the stock. The difference between the actual outgoings and the replacement cost (which would be higher than current costs in the usual situation of rising prices) would be entered in a Replacement Reserve. The latter account indicates, in effect, the extent to which the net assets of the business have been increased in monetary value to account for the rise in price levels. The effect of costing at replacement cost in a period of rising prices is to reduce the profit available for distribution and thus help to maintain the capital employed in terms of purchasing power. The philosophy inherent in the system, which has much to commend it under modern conditions, is discussed more fully in another chapter.

6. Standard cost

A glance at the examples given above shows that each of the major conventions examined produce different material costs, different stock values and hence different figures of profit. Each convention has something to offer – simplicity in the case of first-in, first-out; a smoothing effect with average cost; an approach to current values for last-in, first-out; and the attractive philosophy that all resources must be replaced in the case of the replacement costing method. But each convention produces anomalies and, in the case of the last two, considerable complications in accounting. The one method which, in the opinion of the author, has the potential to overcome these defects is the use of standard material costs. This opinion merely follows that of many eminent authorities and has the perhaps more decisive justification that standard costs are used by the large majority of progressive companies. That is not to say that they are incapable of being misused.

Standard costing is discussed in more detail in a succeeding chapter. So far as material costing is concerned the

practical merits of standard costing may be summarized b
saying that:

(a) It produces consistency of accounting and costin
data; and
(b) It highlights those expenses which are not conformin
to assessed standards.

If standard costing were applied to the transaction
previously considered in relation to other systems, and
assuming that the standard price was set at £410, the store
account would appear as follows, irrespective of the actua
price paid for each consignment of material:

week no.	additions			withdrawals		balance	
	price	quantity	£	quantity	£	quantity	£
10	£410	10	4,100			10	4,100
12	,,	6	2,460			16	6,560
14				8	3,280	8	3,280
				6	2,460	2	820
16	,,	5	2,500			7	2,870
					£5,740		

The justification for using a standard price for the valuation of material costs and of stocks held, is that the
standard is the price at which the business should be able
to buy the materials in the market, having regard to the
economies obtainable through efficient buying. Efficient
buying involves, amongst other factors, obtaining trade
discounts for bulk purchases, but the extent to which orders
of sufficient size can be placed on suppliers depends on

economic stocking policy; and stock policy in turn depends on the production programme. Thus all standards are to a considerable extent inter-connected.

The ascertainment of a standard price for materials which are not of a specialized nature is not normally a difficult exercise, and is generally accomplished by obtaining quotes from the available suppliers. The real management problem which arises in connection with material price standards is to decide the period over which the standard price is expected to be applied. Quotations from suppliers will produce a picture of the current prices obtainable. If the best obtainable price is used as a standard, and the material is likely to be required over a term of years, the standard may soon become outdated by price increases. There are three possible solutions to the problem of rising material prices. In the first place, the price current at the point when the standards are established could be used until the time comes for a general revision of standards. Meanwhile, any price increases in the interim could be written off and treated as revision variances, i.e., caused by deficiencies in the standard awaiting revision. The second device, if it is possible, is to enter into long-term contracts at a fixed price, which may be higher than the current price; but long-term contracts are frequently subject to a 'rise and fall clause' in respect of price. Lastly, an average price likely to cover the period before the next revision of standards could be assessed, probably on the basis of past evidence as to the trend of prices of the material concerned. The latter approach has the merit that it will help to ensure that the standard price used for material is reasonably close to current prices, taken over a reasonable term, possibly twelve months. The stability of accounting information and the reflection of trends in the costing data will be impaired if standards are amended too frequently.

The substitution of a notional but, hopefully, a realistic standard price for the actual price charged by the supplier necessitates the difference being recorded in the accounts as a 'variance'. It is the major variances which should represent the focus of attention by management, not the so-called 'actual costs' which, at least in the case of material costs, depend on the adoption of a particular accounting convention for the pricing of issues.

3 Overheads

The essential costing problems; Variable and non-variable overheads; Analysis by functions; Overhead rates and stock valuations; The 'recovery' of overheads; Determining the overhead rate; The philosophy of the standard rate; Relevant costs and apportionments; General conclusions

The essential costing problems

The word 'overheads' is a very generalized term which covers an immense variety of business expense. For most costing purposes the word may be treated as synonymous with indirect costs, meaning those expenses which cannot be conveniently applied to cost units without some more or less arbitrary process of apportionment. Thus, one considers that the material incorporated into the product for sale is a direct cost, whilst the rent of the premises in which the manufacturing process takes place is treated as an overhead or indirect cost. Because, however, overheads contain so many quite dissimilar elements, it is unlikely that they can be considered as a whole in any precise and searching system of control, so that one of the purposes of this chapter is to discuss the manner in which this large and important volume of expense can be analysed effectively.

Another question of great importance in any costing system is the extent to which, and the manner in which, overheads should be applied to unit costs. Indeed, there is a question as to whether they should be so applied at all. In considering this question it is necessary first to decide the objectives of the exercise. The objectives of overhead costing need to be related to the objectives of costing itself. In an earlier chapter it was suggested that the objectives of costing were twofold: firstly, to provide a system for valuing work in progress and stock as part of the process of ascertaining profit; and secondly, to aid managers in forward planning and control of the enterprise. If, in the course of valuing stocks it is found that different products should logically bear different proportions of overhead cost, then the exercise of applying overheads will also provide information as to the relative profitability of the products or services and thus assist management in allocating resources in the most profitable directions.

In many businesses the process of applying overheads to unit costs, and the mechanics by which the operation is carried out, have become so much a matter of routine, that the truth of the resultant figure tends to be accepted without question. Meanwhile the proportion of business expense represented by overheads increases, and threatens to continue to increase, with mounting investment in plant, systems, control procedures, checking functions, planning operations, training, data-processing and other 'nonproductive expenses'. Some great undertakings apply to unit costs an overhead rate of 300% or 400% on labour costs and continue to concentrate their control effort on direct costs. What is even more alarming is to find a pricing system rigidly chained to the 'full cost' produced as a result of such an exercise in multiplication.

The mechanical process of applying overheads to unit costs usually consists of adding a percentage to some element of direct costs, probably the most widely used being a percentage calculated on direct labour costs. This device has the merit of simplicity, but that appears to be its only merit. It seems odd to find that a job has cost more in overheads as a direct result of a wage award. Other widely-used methods are: percentages on direct materials; percentages on total direct costs; rates per labour hour, machine hour, process hour or operating hour.

The key to the selection of a base to which the rate is applied should logically be to find the factor which causes the overheads to increase or decrease. The ideal is unattainable because some items of overhead, consumable stores, for example, move in relation to the rate of output, and these E. J. Broster* calls 'product variable'; others move in relation to time, such as rent, these being called 'time variable' by the same author. As a generalization some aspect of time seems to be most appropriate, as a base for charging overheads, for even increases in output are to a large extent dependent on time. For this reason, rates per labour hour, machine hour or process hour are often used. In deciding which time factor is most relevant, the key operation of the business is likely to be decisive. Thus in an assembly or fitting shop overheads would probably be best applied as a rate per labour hour; in processing, such as heat treatment, a rate per process hour would be suitable. Individual rates are frequently calculated for key machines or groups of machines where the centre of the work consists of machining.

In other than manufacturing businesses the key function again frequently decides the base for the rate, which is often some measure of the service provided, and for this purpose two factors may be combined. In passenger transport a rate per passenger mile and for the carriage of goods a rate per ton mile, are common. Airways may use the flying hour or, in a more sophisticated system, a rate per capacity ton mile, being the cost of carrying a ton for a mile assuming the aircraft is operated at capacity.

In some commercial undertakings it is found convenient to calculate rates based on some physical measure of the key resources. Multiple stores may calculate the cost of a measurement of counter space; restaurants may calculate a cost per table; and in farming the cost per acre is widely used.

So far as unit costing is concerned, the problems relating

* An article in the *Accountant* on Costing.

to overheads are largely concerned with the question of how and to what extent they are to be applied to the units being costed. Before considering the mechanics and the philosophy behind this process it will be desirable first to discuss the kinds of expense which make up the overheads of a business or of a function of a business.

Variable and non-variable overheads

In Chapter 4, 'The Concepts of Cost', the validity of the common classification of business expenses into their variable and non-variable (or 'fixed') headings is discussed. As a generalization it is suggested, firstly, that this broad division refers to the short term only, because in the long term all expenses must be related to the volume of activity; secondly, it is suggested that any such division will be necessarily imperfect and to a certain extent arbitrary, because business expenses increase and sometimes decrease owing to a wide variety of factors, affecting the various items of expense in different degrees. Nevertheless, and subject to its imperfections, the initial broad classification of overheads into their variable and non-variable categories can be helpful, if only because many of the day-to-day decisions of managers refer to the short term.

(a) NON-VARIABLE EXPENSES. It may be convenient to regard the body of non-variable expenses which exists in every business as derived initially from a pool of resources which must be created to enable the operations to be carried on. These resources will be increased and sometimes decreased in stages, so as to meet plans for expansion or contraction. For example, a business needs to be housed in a building which, whether it is bought freehold or rented, will be a source of continuing expense; most businesses need plant and equipment which need maintenance and, eventually, replacement. In addition there will be a need for a nucleus of policy makers and decision makers – the managers – who will also represent a continuing expense.

If this viewpoint is correct, then it means that non-variable overheads are fixed in relation to the planned utilization of capacity. The resources will be increased or decreased as from the replanning stage when more or less capacity is required or there is an intention to make greater or less use of existing capacity. During the periods between the replanning stages these expenses will not be 'fixed' in the sense that they are unchangeable, because they may rise or fall to a degree, due to influences external to the business, such as a general rise in prices or unavoidable price increases in specific resources.

The exercise of segregating the non-variable overheads is not therefore an *ad hoc* process of running through a list of the business expenses and trying to decide which are likely to remain static in relation to changes in output, but of deciding what resources are required to carry out the long-term forward plans of the business. In attempting this segregation it is likely that some expenses will need dividing into their variable and non-variable elements. Thus it might appear that for the long-term planned activity a transport fleet of a certain number of vehicles is required and the cost of maintaining this fleet will constitute the non-variable expense. Temporary additions (such as by contract hire) to meet short-term variations in activity will incur expenses which should be treated as variable. Likewise it is necessary to segregate the basic resource in administrative staff, technical staff and supervisors, from temporary additions.

It is wise to bear in mind that the total of non-variable expense, when considered in a short period such as a year, will itself be divisible into those expenses which represent a cash outflow during the year, and those which are *apportioned* to yearly periods and do not represent a cash outflow in a particular year. The latter category covers the replacement of wasting assets, such as plant, machinery, fixtures, etc, which are apportioned to years (and, of course, shorter periods) by means of the depreciation charge. The problem as to whether depreciation should be calculated on historical cost or replacement remains a matter of controversy. Since cash flow has rightly become so vital a consideration for management there will be many occasions when the cash element of a cost will need to be segregated from the non cash element, that is, the part which consists of money which was spent in previous periods or (taking the replacement viewpoint) which is not to be spent until some time in the future.

Whether depreciation is based on historical cost of the asset or, less commonly, on estimated replacement value, the amount apportioned to a year would appear to be the only true 'fixed expense' of business, since it results from the spreading forward of a fact – the money originally spent on the asset – or (from the other viewpoint) the spreading back of a fixed amount, the estimated replacement cost. However the amount apportioned to a particular year is dependent on the estimated useful life of the asset. This life could alter for two reasons: firstly, because greater use was made of the asset, such as by overtime working or more than normal mileage covered by a vehicle; secondly, because, due to developments in technology external to the business, it becomes obsolescent earlier than expected. In theory the depreciation charge should be increased in both situations. To the extent that the increase in the depreciation charge is due to abnormal activity, presumably of a temporary nature, the increase should be regarded as a variable expense. More rapid obsolescence might reasonably be regarded as an exceptional charge to be excluded from costs altogether. In practice, however, and particularly where depreciation charges are conservatively assessed, it is unlikely that any change will be made to the charge unless the increased utilization or the obsolescence is severe.

(b) VARIABLE EXPENSES. The problems involved in the segregation of the non-variable expenses, of which a few but by no means all, are outlined above, suggest once again that the result will be an approximation and a generalization which will furthermore be dependent on the conventions used, e.g., the method of depreciation and the elimination of exceptional charges. Once, however, the items which comprise the non-variable expense have been decided, then the remaining body of expense must necessarily fall into the variable category. If, in a particular situation it is considered desirable to subdivide variable expenses, they may be further classified into the two divisions of (a) directly variable in relation to output, and (b) semi-variable. Directly variable expenses largely comprise the direct costs of direct labour and direct materials. So far as indirect or overhead expenses are concerned, fairly typical examples are indirect materials and power in the works, and perhaps commission and carriage. Because of continuing improvements, or at least changes, in the day-to-day operations of business, and because of extraneous influences, such as price changes, it is unlikely that any item of overheads is strictly variable. All that can be said is that one of the jobs of operating management is to endeavour to *make them* variable in relation to output. This desirable aim is unlikely to be applicable to every item of expense but might be more realistically applied to the totality of the variable expenses in a workshop, office or other integral field of activity.

The conclusion to be drawn from the above is that the much advocated division of overheads into their variable and non-variable elements is necessarily somewhat arbitrary. The classification can undoubtedly be useful as a broad guide to some short-term decisions and should then be used with awareness of its imperfections. When this conclusion is applied to the exercise of arriving at a unit cost, whether of a job, process or a product, a decision must be made as to whether the costing is designed to reflect the short-term or the long-term view; if the latter then all costs should be treated as essentially variable.

The analysis by functions

The broad analysis discussed above is between those overheads which are variable in relation to activity and those which do not vary in relation to activity in a particular

T–C

period. It has been suggested that this analysis is subject to
some important qualifications. The importance of discussing
these qualifications is that managers shall appreciate the
implications and the limitations of a unit cost which includes
an overhead rate. This overhead rate may reflect variable
expenses only or may cover both variable and non-variable
expenses, depending on the purpose for which the unit cost
has been calculated, and depending on the time period
contemplated.

In addition to this broad form of analysis it is also desirable to analyse the overheads by what is here called functions. The purpose of such an examination is to decide the
extent to which, for a particular purpose, the overhead rate
should reflect the expenses incurred by a particular function

The major functions will vary according to the nature of
the business. In a manufacturing business it may be said
that the major functions are as follows:

1. Research and development
2. Production, including supply and material control
   (although the latter, here shown as a subsidiary function, may be considered a major function in its own
   right in some concerns)
3. Marketing, including warehousing, distribution, selling
   research and planning
4. Accounting and control, including costing
5. Central administrative services, which may include
   personnel, data-processing and the computer, security
   central filing, typing, mailing and telephone service
6. Headquarters, representing a planning and control
   function, and including the Board and Secretary's
   department and, with a group of companies, central
   executive management

One further expense, which is common to all industrial and
commercial undertakings, is the cost of finance, although
this expense is not normally reflected in unit costs.

In a non-manufacturing business which sells a tangible
product, the basic functions will be analogous to the above

bject to some modifications of emphasis and title. In a
usiness providing a service there is usually to be found a
ain function which organizes and produces the service for
le.

Within each function, in a given period of time, there will
e expenses of both a variable and a non-variable nature, but
ese terms are usually related not to the output of the business
a whole, but to the activity of the function concerned. This
ctivity will be represented by the key factor of the function.
hus, the activity of a buying department may be appropri-
ely measured by the number of orders to be placed in a
eriod, that of the sales department by the number of calls
be made, and so on. In many cases, such as central ser-
ces and accounting, the only convenient measure of activity
frequently the direct expenses of the operating function.

The overhead expenses within each function may be
nsidered under two headings: those which arise within the
unction or department, such as the salaries of the personnel;
nd those which arise because of the use by the function of
e general resources of the business. Following the dis-
ussion on the nature of variable and non-variable expenses,
is reasonable to take the view that expenses derived from
e use of the resources of the business, e.g., the occupation
f space in buildings, are of a non-variable nature, and those
hich arise within the department are of a variable nature,
far as that department is concerned.

If it is considered desirable to collect the total overheads
ttributable to a department, then the non-variable expenses
ill need to be apportioned to that department. Thus it may
e said that part of the cost of the accounts department is a
roportion of the building occupation expense, comprising
ent (or interest on capital) heating, lighting and building
aintenance. The division would probably be carried out on
e basis of floor space. Whether anything is gained by
aking such apportionments is a debatable point. One
eason for making them is to ensure that the correct expense
f a particular service is allocated fairly between the various
roducing departments so that an overhead rate can be

applied to the direct costs arising in that department. Th
cost of the output of the producing department could the
be analysed by the different functions which contributed t
the total expense.

In many businesses no such complicated system of appor
tionments as outlined above is made and management is con
tent with an overhead rate applied uniformly to all operation
and products. This overhead rate simply represents a so
called 'recovery' of all relevant overheads of the business.

Overhead rates and stock valuations

One of the points which has been reiterated in this book –
perhaps to the point of tedium – is that a product cost or an
sort of unit cost must vary according to the purpose fo
which it is to be used. One major purpose for which uni
costs are produced is to value work in progress and finishe
stock as an essential element in the accounting process c
ascertaining profit. For this purpose alone managemen
needs to decide the extent to which variable and non-variabl
overheads should be reflected in overhead rates; also th
extent to which the cost of the various functions of business
as outlined above, should be reflected in those rates.

If one takes, for the sake of argument, the wholly theoreti
cal situation where the activity and the stock (which fo
simplicity can be taken to include work in progress) is un
changed in volume from period to period, then it is quit
irrelevant for the purpose of profit ascertainment what over
heads are included in the overhead rate. A qualification t
this generalized statement, which admittedly removes i
further from reality, is that the overheads must remai
unchanged in amount so that the overhead rate is constant

Assume a situation where a business maintains an activit
represented by 100,000 labour hours a year, costing £1 a
hour, material is on free issue and the product is sold at £
a unit, each unit taking one hour to complete. Variabl
overheads are £100,000 and non-variable overheads ar
£200,000 in a year. Stock is maintained at 20,000 units.

Example 1(a) STOCK IS VALUED AT DIRECT COSTS PLUS
VARIABLE OVERHEADS ONLY

	Year 1	Year 2
Sales: 100,000 @ £5	£500,000	£500,000
Less: cost of goods sold:		
stock at beginning:		
20,000 units @ £2	£40,000	£40,000
production costs:		
100,000 @ £2	200,000	200,000
	£240,000	£240,000
Deduct: stock at end	40,000	40,000
cost of goods sold	£200,000	£200,000
gross profit on sales	£300,000	£300,000
Less: non-variable overheads	200,000	200,000
net profit	£100,000	£100,000

Example 1(b) STOCK IS VALUED AT DIRECT COSTS PLUS
FULL OVERHEADS

	Year 1	Year 2
Sales: 100,000 @ £5	£500,000	£500,000
Less: cost of goods sold:		
stock at beginning:		
20,000 units @ £4	£80,000	£80,000
production costs:		
100,000 @ £4	400,000	400,000
	£480,000	£480,000
Deduct: stock at end	80,000	80,000
Cost of goods sold	£400,000	£400,000
net profit on sales	£100,000	£100,000

Consider now the comparison where, in the second yea
sales are increased by 10%, i.e., by 10,000 units, and stoc
are correspondingly reduced.

Example 2(a) STOCK VALUED AT DIRECT COSTS PLU
VARIABLE OVERHEADS

	Year 1	Year 2
Sales @ £5	£500,000	£550,00
Less: cost of goods sold:		
stock at beginning	£40,000	£40,00
production costs	200,000	200,00
	£240,000	£240,00
Deduct stock at end	40,000	20,00
cost of goods sold	£200,000	£220,00
gross profit	£300,000	£330,00
Less: non-variable overheads	200,000	200,00
net profit	£100,000	£130,00

Example 2(b) STOCK VALUED AT FULL OVERHEADS

	Year 1	Year 2
Sales @ £5	£500,000	£550,00
Less: cost of goods sold:		
stock at beginning	£80,000	£80,00
production costs	400,000	400,00
	£480,000	£480,00
Deduct stock at end	80,000	40,00
cost of goods sold	£400,000	£440,00
net profit	£100,000	£110,00

If, on the other hand, sales were reduced by 10,000 units ₃ the second year, the comparison would be as follows:

xample 3(a) STOCK VALUED AT DIRECT COSTS PLUS ΛRIABLE OVERHEADS

	Year 1	Year 2
Sales @ £5	£500,000	£450,000
ess: cost of goods sold:		
stock at beginning	£40,000	£40,000
production costs	200,000	200,000
	£240,000	£240,000
Deduct stock at end	40,000	60,000
cost of goods sold	£200,000	£180,000
gross profit	£300,000	£270,000
ess: non-variable overheads	200,000	200,000
net profit	£100,000	£70,000

xample 3(b) STOCK VALUED AT FULL OVERHEADS

	Year 1	Year 2
Sales @ £5	£500,000	£450,000
ss: cost of goods sold:		
stock at beginning	£80,000	£80,000
production costs	400,000	400,000
	£480,000	£480,000
Deduct stock at end	80,000	120,000
cost of goods sold	£400,000	£360,000
net profit	£100,000	£90,000

The conclusions to be drawn from the above exercise ma
be summarized as follows:

1. Where overheads, sales, stock and activity is static, tl
   extent to which overheads are applied to unit costs
   irrelevant for the purpose of profit ascertainmer
   provided the method of applying the overheads
   consistent, period by period.

   In this situation, however, a valuation of stock wi
   full overheads will result in a higher figure of capit
   employed than if only part of overheads are so applie
   thus the *percentage* profit on capital employed will I
   lower.

   If the adoption of either approach to costing
   incorrectly interpreted, and costs influence produ
   prices, the company's pricing policy can be adverse
   affected.

2. Where sales increase and stocks decline, the applicatic
   of full overheads to cost units will produce a low
   figure of profit than the application of variable ove
   heads only.

3. Where sales decline and stocks increase, the applic.
   tion of full overheads will produce a higher figure
   profit than where only variable overheads are applie
   Thus the greatest dangers occur to a company usir
   a full overhead rate when sales decline. Stocks w
   tend to be overvalued in a declining market an
   the high profits may lead to excessive dividend pa
   ments.

The 'recovery' of overheads

Businessmen, especially in manufacturing organization
frequently refer to 'the recovery' of overheads. This e>
pression is used to describe the extent to which the overheac
of the cost centre concerned have been applied in a give
period to the output of that cost centre. Assume in a costin

period of a month the overheads applicable to, say, an assembly shop were estimated at £50,000; they were applied to output by means of a rate per man hour; the estimated total man hours in the month were 25,000, and an overhead rate of £2 an hour was established. Assume, further, that in fact only 20,000 man hours were generated in a particular month and the actual overheads for the period were, say, £45,000. The under-recovery would be as follows:

Actual overheads incurred	£45,000
Overheads recovered: 20,000 hours @ £2	40,000
Under-recovery	£5,000

In other circumstances, such as when the output was in fact greater than estimated or the overheads less than estimated, an over-recovery could occur.

It is customary to consider an under-recovery as reflecting adversely on operational management and the converse with an over-recovery; but both of these judgements can be quite unjust as will appear from the following discussion.

Differences between the amount of overheads 'recovered' and the actual overheads incurred may be due to one or a combination of the following factors:

1. Errors in the original estimates of both overheads and activity;
2. Changes in the efficiency with which the work is carried out. Thus, in the above example, it is possible that, owing to increased speed of working, the required output of products was in fact produced but it took only 20,000 hours as compared with the estimated 25,000 hours. In such a case operational management deserves congratulation rather than censure;
3. Changes in overhead cost beyond the control of the manager concerned;

4. Changes in the basis of apportioning overheads to the cost centre.

At this point it is desirable to consider the purpose of the exercise of applying an overhead rate. Is this purpose really to 'recover' all the overheads of the business and of each individual cost centre in the business? If this is in fact the purpose, then it can be said positively that the arithmetical exercise of applying overhead costs to cost units by some rate or percentage does not recover those costs. All it does is to add them to the value of stock and work in progress and to defer charging them against income until the product is sold. In the strict sense of the term there is no real recovery of costs until the customer pays for the goods or services supplied to him. Thus we conclude that in the present context the word 'recovery' is a misnomer.

The answer to the question posed above can, it is suggested, be found by reverting to the purposes of accounting generally. One of these purposes is to present a true and fair view of the profitability of a business on a consistent basis from year to year. One of the principles which govern that objective, although it has many qualifications in practice, is to match expenditure against the income which that expenditure produces. Following that principle it will be necessary to defer the charging of some costs to a period well after they have been incurred and until the point when they are producing income. The application of overheads to unit costs is part of the process of deferring costs for the reasons given above. In short, the cost, including relevant overheads, of production unsold, called stock, is withheld from the current profit and loss account to be charged when the stock is sold.

If this viewpoint is correct, it means that the objective of applying overheads to cost units is to assist in the process of presenting a true view of profit. In furthering this objective it is important that no more values shall be carried forward as stock to a future period of account than are likely to be relevant to future sales. If the attempt is made to 'recover' all the overheads in a period of reduced activity, then the values carried forward are likely to be excessive. In other words the objective of the calculation of an overhead rate is not to 'recover' the overheads at all. It may be that by coincidence full recovery is also associated with the presentation of a true and fair view of profit, but this will only be where the business is operated with ideal efficiency and the estimated overhead rate reflects this desirable but unattainable state of affairs. A more realistic viewpoint is that overhead under-recoveries are to be expected, and that these amounts represent the cost of managerial errors or inefficiency which must be written off against the income of the period when they are incurred. Inefficiency may be represented by uneconomic spending on overhead facilities, idle facilities, inefficient direct operations and a host of other causes; these costs certainly do not represent values to be carried forward to the future.

In the preceding section, consideration was given to the effects on short-term profits of charging (a) variable overheads and (b) full overheads, including their non-variable elements. The illustrations reflected the influence of different levels of sales turnover on the two systems of overhead costing. One interesting conclusion from this presentation was that the inclusion of non-variable overheads can produce irrational variations in the trend of profitability as shown by the accounts. Clearly this was a short-term viewpoint, for given a sufficiently long term, effectively all but an insignificant amount of costs will be charged against sales and the precise method of costing used will be irrelevant. However, modern management demands indications of profit at monthly intervals, whilst more precise statements must be drawn up at yearly periods; all these are short term presentations.

The following examples are now intended to present a further development of the argument that the inclusion of non-variable overheads can distort the trend of profitability where changes in activity occur. In the following examples the change in activity consists of an increase in the output produced, not of the sales.

Using the basic data of the preceding section, it is apparent
that where only strictly variable overheads are charged to
cost units, the *gross profit* per unit will remain unaffected by
increases in output, i.e., on 100,000 units sold the gross
profit will remain at £5 — £2 = £3 a unit or £300,000 in total.
If, however, sales are increased, and therefore gross profit
increased proportionately, the effect of writing off the fixed
amount of non-variable overheads of £200,000 will cause
the rate of *net profit* per unit to rise. So much represents
common experience. The only qualification is also a matter
of common experience: that after a certain increase in
turnover the non-variable costs will also tend to rise until
they themselves become variable.

Consider now the situation when sales remain static but
production output increases to 120,000 units. Such a situation might be deliberately brought about by the prospect of
increased sales in the following year. A similar effect will be
produced if sales fall and output remains static.

Charging a variable overhead rate only, the position will
be as follows:

Sales: 100,000 @ £5		£500,000
Less: cost of goods sold:		
stock at beginning		
20,000 @ £2	£40,000	
production: 120,000 @ £2	240,000	
	£280,000	
Deduct stock at end		
40,000 @ £2	80,000	
cost of goods sold	£200,000	
gross profit	£300,000	
Less: non-variable overheads	200,000	
	£100,000	

hus, the net profit remains unaffected by the increase in
utput, the increase in variable overheads of £40,000 being
arried forward to the next period of account.

If, however, the full rate of overheads of £4 a unit is
harged, the effect will be as follows:

Sales: 100,000 @ £5	£500,000
Less: cost of goods sold:	
stock at beginning	
20,000 @ £4	£80,000
production: 120,000 @ £4	480,000
	£560,000
Less: stock at end: 40,000 @ £4	160,000
	£400,000
apparent profit	£100,000

So far, exactly the same profit as in the first example has
esulted and it is also the same profit as would have appeared
f production had not increased from 100,000 units to 120,000
inits. However, the overheads which in fact could have been
xpected to have been incurred in the year are:

ariable overheads: 120,000 units at £2	£240,000
ion-variable overheads (assumed unaltered)	200,000
actual overheads incurred	£440,000
But, there has been charged to production	480,000
Giving an over-recovery of	£40,000

Conceivably this over-recovery could be carried forward to
e credited against future years' income but more normally

it would be credited to the profit and loss account of the current year, with the following result:

apparent profit, as above	£100,000
Add: overhead over-recovery	40,000
	£140,000

Purely as a result of different methods of costing overheads, profit has been shown at 40% greater than under the first system of costing variable overheads only. The question is: Which is the right method? Or, more specifically; Which rate of overheads was nearer the truth? An attempt to answer this important question will be formulated at the end of the next section.

Determining the overhead rate

The end product of the analysis of overhead expenditure, so far as the formal costing system is concerned, is the application of an overhead rate to the direct cost of the jobs, operations, processes, etc, being carried out in the business, with the final objective of valuing the stock for sale. The actual process of determining the overhead rate in a business which contains many different operations and a diversity of products can be highly complex. Because the truth tends to become hidden in a maze of complexities, it is all the more necessary that an attempt should be made to clarify some major principles.

It should be borne in mind that because goods are being put into stock and sold more or less continuously throughout the year, the overhead rate or rates must be determined in advance of the operations. The first step in the exercise is to decide on the base to which the eventual overhead rate shall be applied. In the simplest forms of costing the base could be the direct cost or even the weight of the eventual product, but this will produce a very crude measure of cost indeed, where different products utilize overhead facilities in different degrees. A more reasonable principle is for the base to represent the key measure of the activity in a workshop, such as the volume of its output expressed in quantity where the output is uniform or, more likely, by some measure of the time planned to be spent on producing a given volume of output. Thus, in many cases, overheads are applied as a rate per standard man hour, process hour or operating hour. The merit of such a base is that many overhead expenses move in relation to time.

The next decision which needs to be made is to determine the extent to which the overhead expenses of the business shall be applied to unit costs. In an earlier section of this chapter the dangers of applying full overheads were illustrated. Nevertheless with a tendency for overheads to move towards the non-variable category, at least in the short run, the elimination of the latter costs from the overhead rate will tend further to divorce the costs from the price. This will make it more difficult to appraise the relative profitability of the various products. The dilemma is quite fundamental.

The solution which is operated by many businesses is something of a compromise. In general a manufacturing business, especially when it is operating in a competitive market, applies to unit costs only those overhead expenses which are directly concerned with the manufacturing operation; thus marketing and general administration expenses are excluded from the calculation. This is not to say that in calculating a cost as a base for price determination, the overheads other than manufacturing are ignored; we are here concerned with the costing *system*, which is basically used for the valuation of stock. The exclusion of marketing and general administrative costs from the overhead rate does not leave a rate which consists entirely of variable expenses – the manufacturing costs often include substantial overheads of a non-variable nature, e.g., depreciation of the plant.

It is interesting to note that the method generally used, as described above, was tacitly approved in a document called ED6 (Exposure Draft) issued in May 1972 by the Accounting Standards Steering Committee of the UK accountancy bodies. This document, which has met some criticism defined cost for the purpose of valuations as 'the expenditur which had been incurred in bringing the product or servic to its present location and condition'.

Emphasis was laid on the need for costs to cover not onl material but also 'costs of conversion', the latter being con fined essentially to production costs. The segregation c costs into their fixed and variable categories was considere inappropriate but production overheads should be include in the cost to the extent that they were involved in the conver sion process, with the implication that they might includ an element of fixed overheads. However, the use of onl manufacturing costs will exclude a major proportion of th non-variable overheads of the business, so that the syste described will be half-way between full costs and variable cost

On the basis that all costs, even the so-called non-variabl or 'fixed' overheads, must be made variable in relation t output in the long term, the question is really resolved int a decision as to whether costing is for the long term or th short term.

In most businesses, it is the long-term viewpoint whic prevails and, consequently, non-variable overheads whic are relevant to the product line concerned are included i the calculation of the overhead rate. As illustrated in th preceding section of this chapter, the inclusion of no variable overheads in production costs will tend to produc irrational fluctuations in profits where the level of activi changes in the short term. Accounting mechanics are, how ever, sufficiently flexible for an alert accountant to be ab to smooth out the trend of profits in such circumstance If, in the case of a fall in activity or sales, profits are seen t be too high in a particular year, the overhead rate used fo the valuation of stock and work in progress can be reduce *for the purpose of the final accounts*. This creates a provisio or reserve against the possibility of loss on eventual sales the stock. Where profits in a particular year are initiall shown to be not as high as they should be in relation to rise in turnover, no particular harm will be done as the effe is that the company retains funds for future development. Expediency has justification where rigid adherence to principle produces anomalies.

The foregoing preliminary considerations with regard to the determination of the overhead rate may be summarized as follows:

1. A decision must be taken as to precisely what categories of expense are to be covered by the overhead rate. The theoretical choice between variable and non-variable overheads is not usually followed by business, probably on the sound grounds that all costs are variable in the long run. The usual basis is to apply overheads which are relevant to the operation of producing the goods or services. Finance costs are usually excluded.

2. The base to which the rate is to be applied must be determined. Ideally, this should be the most realistic measure of the activity in the operation concerned.

3. The need to determine the rate in advance of events necessitates the estimation of both future activity and of the relevant overheads.

4. Where the inclusion of non-variable overheads produces irrational fluctuations in profit, *ad hoc* adjustments may be required for the purpose of final accounts.

It is unlikely that the above conclusions, particularly No. 4 above, will satisfy the manager who seeks precision in accounting information, and who is reluctant that so much shall be left to the judgement of the accountant. Cannot more rationality be introduced into the system? The answer to this question, it is suggested, lies in the use and development of standard costing, which is discussed in some depth in the next chapter.

Meanwhile, partly as an introduction to the idea of using a standard overhead rate, we revert to the unanswered question posed at the end of the preceding section: Which was the right rate, £2 an hour or £4 an hour? The difficulties arise from the assumption that there are two kinds of overheads:

(a) those which vary directly in relation to output; and (b) those which remain static and are independent of output. In the short term, experience indicates that this is generally a true statement. Some overheads, such as power for machines and indirect materials, do vary in relation to output; on the other hand, rent, depreciation and basic administrative salaries are independent of output. The examples are, of course, over-simplified to demonstrate a point.

In the examples it was assumed that output could be raised by 20% to 120,000 units without affecting the non-variable overheads. Given this as a fact, the only logical conclusion is that at an output of 100,000 units the facilities represented by the non-variable overheads could not have been fully utilized. That is to say, there were probably at that level of output idle administrative personnel, idle plant and spare space. Thus, all the £200,000 of non-variable overheads were not relevant to the original production of 100,000 units and the cost of the idle facilities should have been written off below gross profit on sales as a 'management loss'.

The charging of only variable overheads to cost units is unusual in business for the reasons mentioned above. It may also be argued that such a system, whilst theoretically elegant, is virtually impossible to operate in an automated factory where the remaining variable overheads are insignificant and extremely difficult to segregate. There are, however, considerable merits in charging only variable overheads in many of the smaller industrial concerns where the greater part of these costs are in fact variable.

In the larger concern, with an extensive investment in machinery, equipment and trained personnel, an overhead rate which embraces all *relevant* costs (whether variable or non-variable) is generally considered to be more reasonable. But it would be foolish to expect that the ideal overhead rate could be established overnight. It will probably not become evident until the plant is working at capacity; and the signs of capacity working are when the non-variable overheads begin to rise. Applying this thought to the last example, if it were established that any increase in output over 120,000

nits would necessitate increasing non-variable overheads,
hen it is reasonable to suppose that an output of 120,000
nits represents capacity working as the plant stands; in
other words there are no idle facilities. This is a somewhat
crude assumption but it may be a workable one. On this
basis the actual overheads are £440,000 and the standard
overhead rate should be $\frac{£440,000}{120,000} = £3\frac{2}{3}$ an hour. The results

or each year may now be redrafted as follows:

YEAR 1

Sales: 100,000 units @ £5		£500,000
Less: cost of goods sold:		
stock at beginning:		
20,000 units @ £3⅔		£73,300
production: 100,000 units		
at £3⅔		366,700
		£440,000
Deduct: stock at end:		
20,000 units at £3⅔		73,300
cost of goods sold		£366,700
gross profit		£133,300
Less: overhead under-recovery:		
actual overheads:		
variable – 100,000 @ £2	£200,000	
non-variable	200,000	
total	£400,000	
Deduct: recoveries	366,700	
under recovery		£33,300
net profit		£100,000

YEAR 2

Sales: 100,000 units @ £5	£500,000

Less: cost of goods sold:

stock at beginning: 20,000 units @ £3$\frac{2}{3}$	£73,300
production: 120,000 units @ £3$\frac{2}{3}$	440,000
	£513,300
Deduct stock at end: 40,000 units @ £3$\frac{2}{3}$	146,600
cost of goods sold	£366,700
gross profit	£133,300

overhead under or over-recovery:
actual overheads:

variable: 120,000 @ £2	£240,000	
non-variable	£200,000	
total	£440,000	
Deduct: recoveries	440,000	
Net profit		£133,300

The above presentation indicates that the true profit which ought to be made on sales of 100,000 units is £133,300. The reason why only £100,000 of profit was made in Year 1 was because idle resources (not cost of goods sold) cost £33,300.

The philosophy of the standard rate

In considering the merits of using a standard rate of overheads, it is desirable to review the objectives of the exercise in relation to the preceding discussion. We may eliminate any idea that costing is aimed at producing a realizable value of the stock. It has been suggested that costing is, in essence, a process of adding values; the word 'values' in this context being used to mean costs which are expected to be recovered when, but only when, the eventual product or service is sold. All this is subject to the sound accounting rule that the process of adding values must stop before the realizable amount is reached.

The first principle is, therefore, that any expenditure which fails to add value, i.e., increase in saleability in the long run, must be eliminated from the costing process. The application of this principle is, it is suggested, the key to the assessment of a standard overhead rate.

The principle implies, firstly, that unnecessary expenditure should be eliminated; secondly, that inefficient buying of the resources which constitute the overheads must be corrected. A useful device for indicating whether an expense is exorbitant is to watch its relationship to a measure of activity which it is designed to serve. Thus the cost of the Personnel and Wages Departments and of the canteen and welfare service can be related quite simply to the numbers of personnel in the business. More sophisticated techniques will be required to appraise the cost of investments made to obtain future income, e.g., training, research and all kinds of development costs.

The next exercise is to calculate the normal level of activity which the business unit has been designed to achieve. The 'normal level of activity, taking one year with another' is approved as a base for the overhead rate by the accountancy bodies' document, ED6, referred to above. This may mean, for example, the number of operating hours or man hours the business is capable of generating with efficient working in a given period, a year being a convenient period for the purpose of the assessment. In a large business such an assessment may be made for each cost centre or workshop for which it is desirable to establish a separate overhead rate

It can be concluded that at a given point in time there is a single overhead rate which is applicable to a business unit and this rate is based on the economic expenditure in overheads necessary to generate the normal capacity output of the unit. This is not to say that in practice a single overhead rate can be expected to remain valid for ever, for in progressive concerns, means are found of increasing capacity utilization and changes in methods may cause a transfer from direct to overhead costs.

The application of this conclusion will mean that over recoveries and, more probably, under-recoveries of overheads would occur frequently because many factors prevent a business operating continuously at its normal capacity level. If the standard overhead rate has been logically assessed on the lines indicated above, an under-recovery will represent the cost of inefficiency, either in the form of over spending on overheads or under-utilization of capacity. The cost of under-utilization is not part of the cost of the jobs which have been done but of jobs which the business has failed to do. Thus, an under-recovery should be written of in the profit and loss account as it occurs, because it is not an added to value to the work in progress.

If, using the example in the preceding sections, it is assumed that (a) there was normal utilization of capacity represented by 100,000 man hours of work, and (b) that the total overheads of £300,000 was at an economic level, then the standard overhead rate is £3 an hour. The statement may now be re-adjusted as follows:

Years	1	2	3	4
SALES IN UNITS	*in thousands*			
activity in man hours & units	100·0	120·0	80·0	80·0
dd: stock at beginning in units	—	10·0	12·0	8·0
	100·0	130·0	92·0	88·0
ess: stock at end in units	10·0	12·0	8·0	48·0
sales in units	90·0	118.0	84·0	40·0
PROFIT STATEMENT				
Sales value @ £5 a unit	£450·0	590·0	420·0	200·0
ess: cost of goods sold:				
direct costs @ £1 a unit	100·0	120·0	80·0	80·0
overheads @ £3 a unit	300·0	360·0	240·0	240·0
	£400·0	480·0	320·0	320·0
dd: stock at beginning @ £4		40·0	48·0	32·0
	£400·0	520·0	368·0	352·0
ess: stock at end @ £4	40·0	48·0	32·0	192·0
cost of goods sold	£360·0	472·0	336·0	160·0
Gross Profit @ £1 *a unit*	90·0	118·0	84·0	40·0

Add/Deduct: over or under				
recovery of overheads:				
overheads incurred	£300·0	340·0	260·0	260·
overheads recovered	300·0	360·0	240·0	240·
	—	(20·0)	20·0	20·
Net profit	£90·0	138·0	64·0	20·

Relevant costs and apportionments

It will be observed that in the above exposition it wa
suggested that under-recovered overheads should be writte
off to the profit and loss account 'below the line' of gros
profit, so as to ensure that they are not confused with th
profitability of the goods actually produced and sold; like
wise, over-recovered overheads were credited 'below th
line'. In the example, these differences consisted exclusivel
of non-variable overheads; in practice, they may also includ
excess expenditure or economies in variable overhead
Because it is impossible in practice to draw a precise dividin
line between variable and non-variable overheads, an
because expenses may change as a result of many factor
other than changes in business activity, it is impossible t
state precisely the amount of the under- or over-recoverie
which are due to changes in activity.

If it were possible to segregate a body of overheads whicl
were strictly variable in relation to output, and to apply onl
those expenses in the form of an overhead rate, then an
under- or over-recoveries would simply represent over- o
under-spending in comparison with the budgets. Gross profi
on sales, after deducting such differences would mov
strictly in relation to sales volume; but, where there we
considerable fluctuations in activity, the subsequent deduc
tion of the non-variable overheads would cause wid
fluctuations in profits.

A further reason for not restricting the overhead rate t
variable overheads derives from the idea that the purpose o

the exercise is to charge to jobs the expenditure which has
added value to them. Values are presumably added not only
by the typical variable costs of human labour, power, etc,
but also, for instance, by the use of machinery and by the
administrative and accounting effort to the exten. that it
exists to aid the production processes. It is at least question-
able whether the selling and distribution effort adds value
to the product, however necessary those functions may be;
likewise the cost of financing and top management activities
are too remote to be considered as added values to particular
product lines.

The argument has thus proceeded from the point made
earlier in this chapter that an overhead rate based on the
attempt to achieve full recovery of all overheads would
produce anomalies. The remedy, it was suggested, was to
calculate a standard overhead rate including non-variable
costs and to write off over- and under-recoveries. It is now
suggested that in the calculation of the standard overhead
rate it is only relevant expenses which should be included,
whether they are in the short term of a variable or non-
variable nature.

The final question is whether, in assessing the overheads
that are relevant as added values to a product line, the total
should include any apportionments of common services, e.g.,
of building occupation costs, administration and accounting.
If reasonable apportionments are not made, then the resultant cost cannot be said to represent a complete picture of
the values which have been added to the product. The real
danger is that a system of apportionments tends to become
so complex that its effects become impossible to analyse.
Furthermore, in time the amounts apportioned to a product
line can become unreal. One approach to overcoming these
dangers is to ensure that no apportionment should be made
which charges a product line with a greater expense than it
would incur if the service were specially bought from outside
the business. Certainly no product line should bear a charge
which is not necessary for its production.

Building occupation costs is a fairly straightforward

example of a body of expense which can be apportioned with some realism. This expense would include rent (a notional rent if the premises are owned), rates, and services such as heating and lighting and maintenance. The basis of apportionment is normally floor space or perhaps cubic capacity of the area occupied by the departments engaged in making the product. Thus, if the production department occupied 60,000 square feet of a factory with a total floor area of 100,000 square feet and the total occupation cost was £300,000 per annum, the production department would be charged 6/10ths of £300,000 = £180,000 per annum, and this amount would form part of its overheads to be allocated by means of a standard rate over the products made in the department. If, however, it could be demonstrated that the same factory area could be obtained for a cost of, say, £150,000 a year, then only the latter figure should be charged. Other services could be apportioned, as appropriate, on such bases as numbers of personnel, direct costs, power points, numbers of documents involved, etc. The cost of some services can be allocated in a less arbitrary manner, e.g., electricity by metering, telephone installations by actual rents.

It is important that once the amount of an apportioned charge has been agreed as relevant and fair it should not be altered unless the use of the services or their unit cost changes. Assume that building occupation costs are currently apportioned on an agreed basis in the following manner:

Function	Area in sq. feet	Apportionment
Production	60,000	£180,000
Sales	20,000	60,000
Service	10,000	30,000
Admin.	10,000	30,000
	100,000	£300,000

f, for some reason, the service function were disbanded, leaving 10,000 square feet of space vacant, it would be quite inequitable for the total to be re-apportioned so that each function had to bear a greater charge. The cost of the vacant space should be treated as a charge against top management and certainly not as an added value to the products.

General conclusion to this chapter

No attempt has been made in this chapter to minimize the problems associated with the application of overheads to products. It is again emphasized that the routine costing system is essentially an accounting technique aimed at producing a consistent and true view of profit within the framework of accounting conventions. It is not, without considerable adaptation, designed to deal with the infinite range of information required by managers in pursuing their responsibilities of forward planning and control. The need remains, however, for the routine system to be formulated on logical grounds, proceeding from a clear view of the objectives of the exercise to a consideration of what costs are relevant to a product line as representing added values. The result should be consistently applied within a business so that the costs of the several products made by that business are comparable and so that a true trend of cost movements is shown in respect of an individual product. Because business is so diverse, and because the situation in a business is continually changing, the costs of making the same product in different businesses is unlikely to be comparable unless uniform methods are adopted in a particular industry.

4 The Concepts of Cost

Introductory: different approaches for different pur-
poses, relevance; Historical costs; Replacement
costs; Marginal costs; Standard costs; Miscellaneous
concepts: imputed cost, opportunity cost, sunk costs,
joint costs, by-products and scrap

Introductory

Because of the wide variety of uses to which cost figures a
applied in business, a number of concepts, or ideas as to th
nature and constituents of cost, have been developed to me
a fair range of these applications. The objective is to calc
late a figure which will be most relevant to the circumstanc
for which it is intended. The terms most frequently used
describe these concepts are: historical costs, replaceme
costs, marginal costs, standard costs, opportunity costs an
imputed costs. There is, unfortunately, a real danger of the
words becoming a kind of professional jargon which lends
spurious mystique and, indeed, an impression of infallibili
to the science of costing. In fact, it is suggested, these word
do little more than indicate the broad lines on which a co
can be calculated to meet a particular need.

It has been suggested that the only concept of cost whic
is universally applicable is the idea of a cost which is releva
to the purpose for which it is to be used. The relevant co
may be a compound of a number of different approaches.
is clearly important that a manager shall understand th
theory underlying the calculation of a cost and, perhap
equally important, that he shall be in a position to state th

basis on which he requires the calculation to be made for his purposes. For these reasons this chapter examines the major concepts of cost in the light of their special merits and deficiencies.

Historical costs

It is convenient to begin with the idea of the historical cost because it was probably the original basis of costing and remains the foundation of many present-day costing systems.

Historical costing is the attempt to evaluate the money which has been, or was assumed to have been, expended in carrying out an operation, process or function within a business, or in providing a service or product for sale. Changes in the purchasing power of money are ignored in calculating the historical cost. It represents the money expended, often a notional amount, but takes no account of the cost of replacing the resources used up in the process; it aims to spread the actual expenditure of the business over the units of output in some rational manner. When expressed as the cost of a unit of output it is generally an average of the expenditure incurred on a production run or during a period of time; the average may be quite different from the cost of the first unit or the last unit produced.

Thus, if a retailer buys a carpet for resale and pays £100 for it, that amount will, on the face of it, represent the historical cost of the carpet to him. In strictness the £100 will only represent the historical cost of the tangible article purchased, and in fact the transaction will involve a number of other expenses, such as those associated with the operations of buying, transport, documentation and storage. But such ancillary expenses will not be easy to quantify in relation to an individual purchase, and they may be treated as overheads to be spread over all purchases during a year or shorter period.

So far as the manufacture of the carpet is concerned, the historical cost of the article would have been made up of a

number of items, but the basic elements could be expressed
as follows:

Price paid for materials used in the carpet	£1(
Allocation of wages paid to weavers and other operatives, based on the time they had spent on making the article	1:
Overheads applied on some rational basis, say labour hours	1(
total cost	£3!

The important question to be answered is the extent to
which these cost figures can be validly applied to any of the
main purposes of costing, which may be summarized a
follows: the valuation of stock; the pricing of the product
the planning and control by managers.

Consider first the use of historical costs for the valuation
of stock which, it will be recalled, is an essential exercise in
ascertaining what is called a true view of the profit made by
a business in a period of time, and of the financial position
at the end of the period. The existing conventions of
accounting prescribe that stock shall be valued at the lower
of (a) cost or (b) net realizable value (which for present
purposes is equivalent to the price obtainable in the market
place). Assuming that the valuation will be made on the
basis of cost, this being lower than the market price, the
question arises: What is cost for the purpose? Is it in fact
the money that was paid out to purchase the raw material
to pay the wages, and to meet a reasonable proportion of
the overhead expenses?

Suppose, in the case of the retailer, he had held the carpet
in stock for a year and meanwhile money had lost value by
10%. It could be said that the cost of the carpet in terms of
the purchasing power of money at the end of the year was
£100 + £10 = £110. Suppose that in the manufacturer's
workshop the operatives were 'going slow' for som

ason so that the wage cost was higher than it need have
en. Should the value which was placed on the manu-
cturer's stock be higher on that account than it would
herwise be? Should the retailer and the manufacturer
th add to their material costs some amount to cover the
sts of storage and the administrative work involved in the
rchase?

Purely dogmatic and conventional, but not necessarily
tional, answers could be given to these questions. At least
may be said that the valuation of stock on the basis of
storical cost could produce inconsistencies in the ascertain-
ent of profit, and of the capital employed, not only from
eriod to period in the same business, but also as between
fferent businesses.

For pricing purposes the justification for the use of his-
rical cost is that, assuming all products can be sold at a
rice equal to cost plus a percentage profit, and that 'cost'
cludes a full 'recovery' of overheads, a profit will result for
e business. Such a crude method of pricing might, how-
ver, produce a price lower than that obtainable in the
arket, with consequent loss of profit, or a price so high as
limit sales or maybe prevent the product being sold at all.
Ve may therefore conclude that historical costing is a very
efficient basis for price determination.

The next question concerns the use of historical costing
r planning and control. C. T. Horngren (*Cost Accounting:
Managerial Emphasis*) says: 'Historical costs in themselves
re irrelevant, though they may be the best available basis for
stimating future costs.' So much for forward planning.
lowever, historical costing can be a guide to management
the control of costs. For example, if the manufacturer of
he carpet found that his labour cost of £12 was greatly in
xcess of past labour costs for a similar product, he would be
varned thereby that labour efficiency may need investigation.
f course there may be many reasons for a rise in labour
osts – the obvious one being a wage award – and if past
osts had also been high, due to inefficiency, the historical
osting system would have given no warning at all. This

somewhat simplified example suggests that historical cost͏
has only a limited use for control purposes.

Replacement Costs

GENERAL CONSIDERATIONS

In certain circumstances it may be desirable to consid͏
what expenses will be incurred in replacing an article o͏
service. Replacement costs are, for example, important ͏
the purpose of estimating for contracts of long duration, ͏
the forward planning of the expenses of an enterprise a͏
in appraising the economics of replacing capital equipme͏
Replacement costs are essentially concerned with the ͏
placement of the resources used up in the producti͏
processes (or, indeed, in the administrative, research a͏
marketing operations) as compared with the original cost ͏
providing those resources.

Continuing by way of illustration, with the manufactu͏
of a carpet, assume a situation where prices were genera͏
rising. In this not uncommon situation it is likely that ͏
manufacturer would have to pay more than £10 to repla͏
the materials used up in making the original carpet; ͏
would also have to pay more to keep his labour force ͏
being, as a result of wage awards; and likewise his overhea͏
in the form of purchased services might well have increas͏
in price. Using notional figures, the replacement cost of ͏
carpet might be compared with the historical cost as sho͏
below:

	historical cost £	replacement cost £
materials	10	11
labour	12	13
overheads	16	18
total	£38	£42

In considering in what circumstances and for what purposes it would be desirable to calculate the replacement cost,
it is again valuable to relate this question to the main
objectives of costing, i.e., planning, controlling, pricing and
valuations.

The formulation of plans for the future involves the
management in deciding between alternative courses of
action. One such decision which could be facing the manufacturer of the carpet might be whether to attempt to reduce
its costs, and thus increase profit, by using a less expensive
material. He finds, however, that because the alternative
material is more difficult to work, its use will increase labour
time, and the resultant costs, on a historical costing basis,
will be as follows:

materials	£ 9
labour	14
overheads	16
total	£39

This cost is now £1 higher than the preceding historical
cost so that the change in material appears to be unjustified.
If, however the comparison were made using replacement
costs the total might be less than the replacement costs with
the old material and, since the manufacturer is considering
future costs, which must be replacement costs, it is the latter
comparison which is valid.

So far as the pricing decision is concerned, the relevant
costs must also be replacement costs since it is the cost of
future sales which is in question. This is not to suggest that
cost ought to dictate price but it will, in association with the
price obtainable in the market-place, indicate whether it is
worthwhile to undertake a business venture. Where, as is
usual, there is a range of prices acceptable in the market, and
demand varies inversely with price, a supplier can be expected to select the price which will maximize his profit. This is
the point where price less cost multiplied by turnover is at a

maximum. Cost will be affected by turnover or activity an
if past costs are used for this purpose they will be misleadir
because they will have been assessed on past activity. A mo
detailed discussion of pricing policy will be found in Taylc
and Palmer's *Financial Planning and Control*, also publishe
in the Pan Management Series.

Another area of decision-making where replacement cos
will be appropriate is the question of the most profitab
product mix. This is largely a question of ensuring th
limited resources are applied to the most profitable activitie
In this sense the limitation on resources may, according t
circumstances, be the supply of skilled labour, specialize
machinery, materials or finance. The costing system reflec
the use of resources in monetary terms and, in an age c
rapid and continuous change, the relationship between th
costs of the resources used in a business will change likewis
Thus there may be occasions when it is cheaper to buy ol
components rather than to manufacture them, or to u
mechanical rather than manual methods. It will be the futu
not the past relationships between costs which will be rel
vant in deciding whether to apply more or less of particula
resources to the production of products or services.

Replacement costing is discussed further in a later chapte

The marginal cost

R. G. Lipsey in *Positive Economics* defines the marginal cc
as 'the difference between the total cost of producing son
rate of output and the total cost of producing at a rate of o
less unit'. In the same book he allies the marginal cost wi
the incremental cost, which he describes as 'the increase
total cost resulting from raising the rate of production I
one unit'. These are fairly standard definitions of margin
and incremental costs from the economist's viewpoint, b
the practical difficulty with these theoretical definitions
that it is almost impossible to quantify the cost of makii
one more unit; or to assess the difference in total cost caus
by producing one less unit. In more general terms, margin

osts may be considered as the additional outgoings incurred
y a business as a result of increasing output. An increase of
ne more unit is not worth consideration in business, even if
could be quantified in money, but it is important for a
usinessman to know how much more money will go out of
ne business as a result of a further production run or other
zeable increase in output over a period.

The applications of marginal costing are numerous, and
re further discussed in a later chapter, but meanwhile it may
e helpful to summarize as follows some common situations
here marginal costs are relevant:

1. To aid decisions as to alternative methods of production;
2. To assess break-even levels and the effect of changes in
   volume on profits;
3. To aid in pricing decisions, particularly where it is
   expedient to price below full cost.

The marginal cost will always be different from the aver-
ge cost of existing or normal output, as reflected in the
onventional costing system. This is largely because the
arginal cost excludes expenses which would have been
curred whether the additional activity took place or not.
a general, the expenses included in a conventional costing
stem may be categorized as follows:

1. Outgoings directly incurred to produce goods and
   services; normally, material incorporated in the product, labour applied to the product, and other variable
   costs such as power and ancillary services to production.
2. Apportionments of continuing overheads, such as rent
   and other occupation expenses, staff salaries and
   generally all those expenses necessary to maintain a
   business organization in being.
3. Apportionments of past investments in productive
   facilities, such as depreciation of plant, amortization of
   leases and past research and development costs carried
   forward.

Essentially, only the outgoings in Category 1 above will

constitute marginal costs. Category 2 is largely expenditure which will continue to be incurred in the short term whether output is increased or not, and Category 3 represents money already spent.

Sometimes marginal costing is referred to as 'direct costing' (especially in America), or as 'variable costing' because the elements which make up the marginal cost largely include expenses which can be directly applied to the product, and also those which are directly variable in relation to output. It is suggested, however, that there is an important distinction between these terms. Marginal cost may, for instance, include those expenses which had been formerly treated as 'fixed', and this will occur when an increase in output necessitates the acquisition of further 'fixed' facilities such as machinery or space.

AN ILLUSTRATION OF MARGINAL COSTING IN PRACTICE

Assume that a business, with capital employed of £100,000, manufactures a homogeneous product which it sells at a price of £10·80 a ton. The business has a normal production capacity of 10,000 tons a year. The budgeted expenses at this level of turnover are:

Production costs		
materials		£16,000
production wages		15,000
production overheads:		
variable	£3,000	
non-variable	6,000	
		9,000
Total production costs		£40,000
Warehousing, distribution and sales expenses		28,000
Administration expenses		32,000
Total expenses		£100,000

The average cost per ton calculated from the above figures
is:

Production	£4·00
Warehousing, distribution and sales	2·80
Administration	3·20
	£10·00

On the basis of these figures each order might be costed as
follows:

		per ton
(a) *For the valuation of stock*		
Production costs:		
direct	£3·10	
overheads @ 60% on direct		
labour	0·90	
		£4·00
Add: (b) *As a basis for pricing*		
Warehousing, etc, at 70% of		
production cost	£2·80	
Administration at 80% of total		
costs	3·20	
		6·00
Total cost		£10·00
Add: (c) For profit		0·80
		£10·80

The rate of profit is 8% on total cost and, since the turnover
rate on capital employed is 1, 8% will also be the rate of
profit on capital employed, assuming all orders are priced at
£10·80 a ton and that costs conform to the estimate.

The management is now offered an additional order for

2,000 tons but the best price they can obtain for this order is only £8 a ton. The question of whether to accept this order or not does not depend on the average cost of existing production of £10 a ton, but on the marginal cost of the additional order (ignoring for the time being several important considerations of marketing and stock-holding policy). The assessment of the marginal cost may be carried out on a unit cost basis but when there is a substantial addition to the output, as in this case, the exercise is more thoroughly conducted by a process of rebudgeting the whole business expense on the following lines:

	existing	additional	total
Output and sales in tons	10,000	2,000	12,000
	£	£	£
Price	10·80	8·00	
Sales value	108,000	16,000	124,000
Production costs			
Notes			
(1) materials	£ 16,000	3,200	19,200
(2) wages	15,000	3,000	18,000
(3) variable overheads	3,000	600	3,600
(4) non-variable overheads	6,000	—	6,000
(5) warehousing, etc	28,000	5,200	33,200
(6) administration	32,000	3,000	35,000
Total expense	£100,000	15,000	115,000
Profit	£ 8,000	1,000	9,000

Notes:
(1) Material costs are treated as strictly variable, although it is possible that the larger scale of purchases would produce greater trade discounts, in which case the material costs of existing production would decrease as well as those of the new order. In fact, the total of the increased discount would be attributable to the new order. Against this possible

advantage might be increases in buying costs caused by sourcing additional materials.

(2) Wages have been treated above as strictly variable but in fact the longer production runs might result in improved labour times overall. Again the whole of such economies are attributable, for present purposes, to the new order. If, on the other hand, the additional order caused additional expense due to overtime working, that expense, on whatever orders it occurred, must be treated as due to the new order.

(3) Variable overheads are shown as the same as previous rates but it might be worth examining these overheads in detail since few service costs are strictly variable.

(4) The example above assumes that none of the non-variable overheads would be affected by the new order but this assumption will only be valid if the facilities were previously under-utilized. If that were the case, then it cannot be said that the new order incurred any non-variable overheads and none should be apportioned to that order, *assuming it was a short run or temporary addition to output.* If the additional output was of a permanent or long-run nature, then it should be charged with the cost of the facilities which it employs, on the grounds that in the long run they could have been applied to some other profitable purpose or, perhaps, eliminated. There would be an inevitable increase in non-variable overheads if the facilities were already being used to capacity, and that increase would be attributable to the new order. Thus it can be a grave error to assume that the marginal cost never includes the so-called 'fixed' or non-variable overheads; all expenses are variable in the long run.

(5) and (6) A small increase has been shown for these expenses to indicate that they include items which are normally variable and some which are normally non-variable. Usually administrative expenses have more resilience to changes in output than do production overheads, no doubt because the latter are closer to the workshop floor.

An important conclusion to be drawn from the above exercise is that the assessment of the marginal cost is in practice a far more complex process than simply segregating variable costs.

The standard cost

Some of the more important techniques derived from standard costing will be examined in a subsequent chapter. For the present review of the various concepts of cost, it may be helpful to discuss the 'idea' which underlies standard costing.

How is the standard cost defined? Unfortunately the writing on the subject offers a somewhat wide variety of definitions. In his book, *Standard Costing*, J. Batty refers to standard costs as predetermined costs, and so does Horngren in *Cost Accounting: A Managerial Emphasis*. Other writers frequently use the word 'yardstick' in relation to standard costs. These expressions do not, however, adequately convey the fundamental change in the viewpoint of costing which occurs when a standard costing system is instituted in place of an historical costing system. The standard cost is what the cost of an operation or service ought to be under given conditions and subject to given conventions of costing. It is thus a notional amount which depends entirely on the conditions predicated. It is this notional amount which is treated as the value of the stock and the cost of the goods sold.

The conditions associated with a standard cost are essentially a standard of efficiency and a level of activity. Using material as an example, the standard material cost of a product implies the purchase of the required quantity of material at an economic price and in economic lots. This in turn implies the existence of a production plan and a storing policy. All the standards inherent in the elements of cost which comprise a product cost or the cost of an operation are interdependent. To carry the argument to the extreme, it could be said that the standard costs derive from the corporate plan.

In the practical affairs of business these theoretical conderations are necessarily qualified and compromised. The search for the ideal standard is like chasing the rainbow's end for which businessmen do not normally have the time and rarely the inclination. The benefits of standard costing can be obtained with standards which are reasonable but not perfect.

All costs are the product of two factors, price and quantity. Thus, the material standard for a job might consist of (a) a usage of 100lbs, and (b) a unit price of £2; giving a standard material cost of £200. Labour costs will consist of the time required to do the job multiplied by the rate payable to the operative. Overhead standards should be based on a study of the facilities and services necessary to sustain the direct operations and having regard to the volume of activity intended. The volume of activity will be a matter of budgeting and thus the standard costing system and the budgetary control system will be integrated.

The fundamental change in the philosophy of costing brought about by the introduction of standard costing is that the convention of the so-called actual cost no longer exists and is replaced by the convention of a standard or notional cost based upon preconceived conditions.

So far as the valuation for work in progress and stock is concerned, the use of standard costs will achieve the principle of consistency from period to period and thus produce a consistent view of profit and of the financial position of the business. The valuations derived from standard costs will be unaffected by inefficiencies, nor will they be inflated by temporary falls in activity. The values of the stocks will depend on the standards used, but any inaccuracies they contain will not affect the trend of profit. However, this statement must be qualified by the fact that standards may need revision from time to time, not only to remedy disclosed inaccuracies in their compilation but also to reflect changing conditions in business.

Because of their general consistency and objectivity, standard costs should be more valuable than historical costs in the determination of price. To the extent that costs have any effect on short-term pricing tactics it is probable tha the standard marginal cost will be most relevant.

It is widely accepted that standard costing achieves i apotheosis as a control mechanism for the use of manager The transformation is effected by the technique of varianc analysis which is further examined in a succeeding chapte Variance analysis is simply the recording and analysis of th differences between the standard cost of a measure of outp and the actual expenses incurred in producing that outpu It is the variances and not the actual expenditure whic should be the focus of management's attention, thus fu filling the old precept of 'management by exception'.

Miscellaneous concepts

Historical costs, marginal costs and standard costs a probably the three most important approaches to costi used in business. None of them is the perfect solution to th many problems of costing and each of them needs using managers with understanding and discretion. As was pro ably evident in the narrative, it is suggested that standa costing is best suited to meet the needs of management. B the technique of using standard costs needs considerab experience and careful interpretation. 'Why,' said the Dod 'the best way to explain it is to do it.' (*Alice in Wonderlana* In connection with the interpretation of cost data the follo ing further concepts are useful to bear in mind.

(a) IMPUTED COST

This term refers to the profit which could be earned assets, including money, by lending or hiring out those asse for interest, royalties or rent. Thus, if money in the ba could be lent or invested at a rate of interest and is instea used to develop a new product line, a cost which can imputed to that product line is the interest foregone. Lik wise there is usually an imputed cost in the use of buildin on the company's business, this being the net rent whic could otherwise be obtained on those buildings. Much th

me applies to plant which could have been leased to some-
e outside the business, or might have earned more income
it were applied to some other work. Except in an extremity,
ch as a severe fall in demand of the products made by the
mpany, it is unlikely that, in fact, a business would lease
t its plant; and if that plant cannot be used profitably, the
st remedy is usually to dispose of it thus saving space and
aintenance costs. Nevertheless, when an imputed cost is
own to exist, that fact needs to be borne in mind by the
anagement when considering the best use of the assets
ncerned.

(b) THE OPPORTUNITY COST

e opportunity cost is related to the imputed cost and is,
ore specifically, the cost of the opportunity foregone. The
pportunity foregone is the prospect of receiving income or
ducing expense by taking one course of action in prefer-
ce to another.

Managers are usually well aware that an opportunity cost
ists in a particular situation but even so may deliberately
ke the less remunerative alternative for reasons of policy.
 simple example which is, however, by no means un-
mmon, is where a business buys material or services from
 particular supplier knowing that that supplier's price is
gher than his competitors' prices. The decision may have
en taken to preserve an alternative source of supply, or to
oid the risk of failure to deliver. Opportunity costs are
ten incurred to reduce risk; if so they may be considered
 the cost of insurance against risk. It would be theoretically
sirable to quantify both the risk and the opportunity cost,
t in most of the day-to-day decisions of business the
sessment of risk would be too lengthy an exercise to be
acticable and too imprecise to be of much value. For day-
-day decision-making managers tend, quite properly, to
ly more upon judgement and experience than complex
ithmetic. Nevertheless, the cost of the opportunity fore-
ne is often susceptible to measurement in monetary terms
 it would be in the case of the supplier's price mentioned

above – and that cost should be borne in mind in making a
significant choice between alternative courses of action.

There are probably many occasions when opportuni
costs are incurred unknowingly because of faulty info
mation about relative costs. An unreasoning faith in hi
torical costs, or an incomplete understanding of margin
costs, may be at the root of many lost opportunities.

(c) SUNK COSTS

This somewhat imprecise expression is commonly used
describe money spent in the past but from which the benefi
are intended to accrue in subsequent periods. In order
match expenditure against income the cost is apportione
over the future years in which the benefit is expected to aris
The obvious example is the cost of a machine which will
productive for many years to come and of which the cost
spread forward in the accounts and costing records by mea
of the depreciation charge. More commonly, the term is use
to describe the investment of money for benefits which a
difficult to quantify, typical examples being research an
development expenditure, the cost of an advertising car
paign to launch a new product, and training costs. Becau
of the difficulty of predicting the income likely to arise fro
the expenditure, it is frequently written off against t
income of the period when it was disbursed. It has been sa
that half of advertising (or research) expenditure is waste
money but no one knows which half.

Some writers maintain strongly that all past costs a
irrelevant for decision-making. Lipsey in *Positive Economi*
brings out this point very clearly when he likens a manag
ment decision to that facing a poker player presented wi
the alternative of betting on his hand or surrendering h
stake. What he has gained or lost so far in the game is qui
irrelevant.

The analogy breaks down, however, when it is applied
a past cost which produces an enduring benefit. The amou
of the expenditure may be irrelevant but the value of t
benefit gained may be a vital factor in business decisio

making. Even the poker player may have gained in experience out of his past losses. In making business decisions management should be aware that future activities will have the benefit of a machine bought years ago; of past technical research; of the customer goodwill created by an advertising campaign; these investments may be unsaleable in the market-place but they may have great value to the business concerned.

Another aspect of sunk costs worth considering is that if the benefit of the past investment is to endure, the asset so obtained will usually need replacement at some time in the future, either due to use, the passage of time or obsolescence. It is illogical to bring into account the sunk cost of a machine when considering future plans, but it will usually be necessary to include in the calculations the estimated cost of replacing the machine. Likewise, the benefits of research and development rarely last for ever and an element of the cost of future production which relies on the research is the cost of keeping it up to date. Thus, it may be concluded that although sunk costs are irrelevant for management decisions, the value to the business of past investments is relevant and so is the need to replace and renew those investments.

(d) JOINT COSTS

Joint costs are those which are incurred in bringing basic material to the condition or location (the 'separation point') from which a number of distinct products are produced from that material. Thus a wide variety of products are made from mineral oil, coal and various chemicals. A particularly interesting example of where joint costs occur is with animal carcasses of which practically the whole will be disposed of, either with little or no further processing, as meat, or by extensive operations to produce leather goods and processed food.

The costing problem is to devise a rational method of allocating the cost of the basic material to the several end-products. The problem arises only where the business producing or acquiring the basic material is the same as that

which manufactures and distributes the end-products.
Where, for example, a business buys hides for the manufacture of, say, handbags, it would not be unduly difficult to
allocate the cost of buying a particular hide to the number
of handbags that are produced from it. Difficulties would
arise, however, where a particular hide was used to produce
a variety of products, say handbags, book-binding material
and cleaning leather. Greater difficulties occur where, for
instance, a food manufacturer buys carcasses for processing
into various meat products; the basic material is not homogeneous and as a result there is no particular logic in allocating parts of the animal on the basis of weight.

A fundamental question which needs to be answered in
these circumstances is: What is the purpose of making the
allocation?

One necessary objective of the exercise is to place a value
on the completed products, and those in course of processing, for entry into the accounts at the end of the accounting
period. As explained earlier, the valuation of work in progress and stocks is an essential part of the accounting process
of ascertaining the profit made by a business in a period, and
of the capital employed in the business.

Another very desirable objective is to calculate the cost of
the sales of each category of product so that their relative
profitabilities may be examined. The examination of relative
profitability must be a primary responsibility of management in order that the resources of the business shall be
deployed in the most efficient and profitable manner. The
allocation of cost to products and the valuation of stock are
integrated processes in a conventional accounting system,
but this is not to say that the methods of allocation used in
the conventional accounts will be appropriate for all
management purposes.

Typical bases for allocating a joint cost are as follows:

(a) On the relative weight or volume of the basic material
    consumed by each end-product. This would be a rational
    basis where the basic material was homogeneous.

(b) On the cost of further processing required by each product. This method would appear to have little to recommend it from the viewpoint of arriving at an objective cost of the product. If the assessed cost was largely the basis of determining price, and the processing costs were small in relation to that of the basic material, this method would produce a high cost, and therefore a high price, for those products which needed considerable processing; but this is pricing, not costing.

(c) On the sales value of the end product. This method is frequently used but its only effect would seem to be to reduce, quite arbitrarily, the profit on high priced products and to increase the profit on those with a low price. If this is so, the result is likely to confuse rather than guide management.

(d) On the saleable value of the basic product or parts thereof. There would seem to be considerable logic in this method which also avoids the inconsistencies of those indicated above. It has a particularly valid application where the product is not homogeneous but it has the disadvantage that it would tend to produce stock values inflated, unless adjusted, by notional profit on the basic material. This method is further discussed below.

Meanwhile it may be useful to examine the effect of using one or other of methods (a), (b) and (c) in relation to the following example:

Assume a situation where 1,000 gallons of a basic material are available at a cost of £600 and, by further processing, three distinct products are produced from this material. Each of the end-products incurs different processing costs and their sales values are not necessarily related to these costs. Process loss is ignored for simplicity.

Other relevant facts are as follows:

product	gallons	processing costs £	sales value £
A	400	560	1,200
B	300	200	600
C	300	40	1,200
	1,000	£800	£3,000

The result of making allocations of the basic material cost of £600 by various methods is shown by the following tables:

product	material allocation £		processing cost £	total cost £	sales value £	profit £	per gal £
1. ON GALLONAGE USED							
A	4/10	240	560	800	1,200	400	1·00
B	3/10	180	200	380	600	220	0·7?
C	3/10	180	40	220	1,200	980	3·2?
		600	800	1,400	3,000	1,600	
2. ON PROCESSING COST							
A	0·70	420	560	980	1,200	220	0·5?
B	0·25	150	200	350	600	250	0·8?
C	0·05	30	40	70	1,200	1,130	3·7?
	1·00	600	800	1,400	3,000	1,600	

ON SALES VALUE

0·4	240	560	800	1,200	400	1·00
0·2	120	200	320	600	280	0·93
0·4	240	40	280	1,200	920	3·07
1·0	600	800	1,400	3,000	1,600	

ON SALES VALUE PER GALLON

3/9	200	560	760	1,200	440	1·10
2/9	133	200	333	600	267	0·89
4/9	267	40	307	1,200	893	2·98
	600	800	1,400	3,000	1,600	

The final alternative, that of assessing a market value for
ısic material consumed by each end-product, would put
e processing operation on the same basis as a business
hich had to buy the material concerned. The resultant
ofit shown by each processing operation would give an
•jective indication as to whether such processing was a
able operation in itself and would show its relative
ofitability in relation to other processes and, indeed, in
lation to notional sales of the base product itself. If the
arket price of the base product was shown to be below the
st of its acquisition or production, then inquiry should be
rected towards the latter costs. If the base material was
·oduced at a cost above its market value, either means
ould be found of reducing the manufacturing costs or, if
at were found to be impossible, it would be more economic
buy out the material. If the base material was bought out
a cost above market value, then clearly inquiry should be
rected at the buying operation. In these ways the method
ggested should provide management with useful data for

ᴄ–E

cost control and the efficient deployment of resources.

On the face of it, the method suggested would offend th
accounting principle that stocks should be valued at th
lower of cost or net realizable value. Thus for final accoun
ing of the business as a whole any profits included in stoc
and work in progress would need to be eliminated, but th
adjustment could be made as a total without affectin
management statements showing the profitability o
individual product groups.

Many businesses in such situations do in fact operat
profit centres on the lines indicated above and others valu
stocks, where joint costing is involved, at net realizab.
values less an estimated profit percentage.

The charging of basic material costs to end-products o
the basis of the market value of that basic material will, a
explained above, give management a picture of the relativ
profitability of the end-products. A further primary co
sideration of management is to find a means of determinin
whether it would be more profitable to sell the base materi:
as it stands than to undertake the further process of pre
ducing an end-product. Such an exercise would be particu
larly enlightening where the profitability of one or more o
the end-products was poor. For the purpose of the exerci:
in its simplest form there is no need to make any allocatio
of the basic material costs to end-products. Using the da
of the previous example, and assuming that the materi
could be sold at a price of £2·10 a gallon, the alternativ
could be expressed as follows:

(a) SELL THE BASIC MATERIAL

Sales: 1,000 gallons @ £2·10	£2,1C
Less: costs	6C
	———
Profit	£1,5(
	═══

b) PROCEED WITH FURTHER PROCESSING

Sales		£3,000
Less:		
cost of basic materials	£600	
cost of processing	800	
	—	1,400
Profit		£1,600

The illustration is over-simplified because, amongst other practical complications, it ignores the possible effect on the general overheads of the business of eliminating the processing operations. If the cost of common services has already been allocated between the basic materials and the end-products, then the elimination of the latter might transfer some overheads to the basic material and reduce the profitability of that material on sale; it is also possible that the opposite effect might occur. If the exercise showed that the most profitable course of action was to sell the basic material as such, it is not suggested that the conclusion is to take that course of action in fact, because this would involve loss of the investment in the processing plant and related facilities. The action indicated is that the costs, prices, volumes and mix of the end-products need investigation.

The next exercise could be to assume that one or more, but not all the end-products, were eliminated, and that the amount of basic material so made available was sold without further processing. Assuming that in the above example the volume of sales of each product cannot be increased, then the alternatives are to examine the position after eliminating a combination of A, B and C. The most profitable combinations will become evident by considering the relative profitability of the different products after charging them with the market price of the basic product.

pro-duct	material costs @ £2·1	processing costs	total costs	sales	profit	per gal
	£	£	£	£	£	£
A	840	560	1,400	1,200	(200)	(0·50
B	630	200	830	600	(230)	(0·77
C	630	40	670	1,200	530	1·77
	2,100	800	2,900	3,000	100	

Add: notional profit on sales of material
    to processing operations   1,500

                                   £1,600

This exercise indicates that only product C has a profit
ability per gallon above that to be achieved by selling the
basic material, and that the business would make more
profit by eliminating products A and B. The figures are as
follows:

Sales:
basic material, 700 gals @ £2·10   £1,47
product C   1,20

                                    £2,67

Less: Costs:
basic material   £600
product C   40

                                        64

Profit   £2,03

The above example assumes, for simplicity, the use of a homogeneous basic material. In such a situation the relative profitability of the various end-products could have been demonstrated by allocating to them the cost of the basic material by proportionate weight or volume used. But that method would not have shown whether sale of the basic material without further processing was more remunerative. What is perhaps of greater importance is that the presentations immediately above could have been made even if the material was not homogeneous and that, as with animal carcasses, parts of it were saleable at varying prices.

The method advocated may be of interest and value to managers in connection with the analysis and determination of price. It is not unreasonable to assume that what the ultimate consumer is paying for is (a) a quantity of basic material which he could get processed if he so wished; and (b) a processing operation. Thus the housewife has the alternative of buying a ready-made steak and kidney pie or buying the ingredients and processing them herself. It is, indeed, quite likely that when contemplating the purchase of the ready-made pie the housewife will make a mental calculation of the price she would have to pay for the various ingredients. The method of charging the market price of the basic material will, in a business, enable not only price but also costs and profit to be analysed between the two elements of the final product. Using product C for illustration, the figures are as follows:

Product C

ANALYSIS OF PRICE, COST AND PROFIT

		per gallon
(i) Basic Material		
Sales: 300 gals @ £2·10	£ 630	£2·10
Less: costs – 3/10ths of £600	180	0·60
Profit	£450	£1·50

(*ii*) Processing

Gross sales	£1,200	£4·00
Less: sales of basic material, above	630	2·10
Net sales of processing	£ 570	£1·90
Less: costs of processing	40	0·13
Profit on processing	530	£1·77
Total profit	£980	£3·27

A similar presentation for product A shows clearly that the price charged for processing is too low in relation to the costs (it may be, of course, that the costs are too high in relation to the price obtainable).

Product A

ANALYSIS OF PRICE, COST AND PROFIT

(*i*) *Basic Material*

Sales 400 gals @ £2·10	£ 840	£2·10
Less: costs – 4/10ths of £600	240	0·60
Profit on material	£600	£1·50

(*ii*) *Processing*

Gross sales	£1,200	£3·00
Less: sales of material, as above	840	2·10
Net sales of processing	£ 360	£0·90
Less: costs of processing	560	1·40
Loss on processing	(200)	£(0·50)
Total profit	£400	£1·00

(e) BY-PRODUCTS AND SCRAP

The distinction between a joint product and a by-product is often by no means clear. Thus gas and chemicals produced from coke may be considered either joint products or by-products. Relative values of sales turnover will clearly influence the description but probably more important is what the management consider to be their main area of concentration. In some cases a by-product has, as a result of changes in markets and technology, become a main product or a joint main product; in other cases the reverse may occur.

Likewise the distinction between by-products and scrap may become blurred if the demand for scrap increases and it rises considerably in value. Apart from such exceptional situations scrap is usually distinguished without difficulty as wastage from a manufacturing process. Familiar examples are sawdust and wood chippings in a furniture manufacturer, ends in a textile mill, and metal scrap from machining operations. In some cases the scrap may be re-used in the same business, in other cases it is sold, and occasionally a payment may have to be made to remove it. The disposal of scrap which is likely to cause pollution has become a significant item of business expense.

The importance of a business distinguishing between joint products, by-products and scrap lies in the accounting methods involved and the effect of those methods on unit costs. As discussed above, the production of joint products usually involves a method of allocating the basic material to the several end-products, if their relative profitability is to be demonstrated. No such allocation is normally involved for either by-products or scrap. It is sufficient if (a) the total cost of the material and services involved in the manufacture of a main product, including the eventual by-products and scrap, is charged to those products, and (b) sales of the by-products and the scrap are credited to that cost. Where a standard costing system is in operation both the costs under (a) above and the sales under (b) above will be applied to the product at standard, variances being extracted in the usual way.

There seems to be no particular advantage to be gained by setting up a system for costing the by-products or the scrap, because the quantities and quality produced will depend on the methods of manufacture of the main product; in fact the quantity and quality of the scrap may vary inversely with the efficiency of the production of the main product. It is, however, clearly desirable that accurate statistics be maintained of the volume of scrap and by-products produced as a check on their output and of the amounts sold.

If it is objected that it is desirable to cost a by-product in order to appraise its profitability, then the inference is that the material is no longer a by-product but has become a joint product. If this is not the case, then it is the profitability of the main product, after crediting by-product and scrap sales, which is in question. Furthermore, there seems to be no logic in costing a by-product in order to value the stock of that commodity for the purpose of the accounts, because the cost of all by-products and scrap produced will already be included in the work in progress, stock or cost of sales of the main product.

If the sales value of by-products is significant in relation to the turnover of the main products, and if there is substantial delay between production of the by-product and its sale, there could be some distortion of the profitability shown by individual contracts and interim accounts. Such profitability would be lower than it should be because of the omission of the credit for by-products and scrap sold. This situation could, however, be avoided by crediting the main product with the sales value of the scrap and by-products as soon as they are produced, and making whatever adjustments are necessary when they are eventually sold.

5   Standard Costing

Introductory: the mechanics, a new attitude to costing, essentially costs of operations, advantages; The mechanics illustrated; The principles of variance analysis; The control of variances; Special variances; Overhead variances

Introductory

The general philosophy of standard costing was introduced in Chapter 4 and this chapter will deal largely with the mechanics of the system. In considering the techniques described in this chapter it should be borne in mind that all systems of costing need to be adapted to the circumstances of the particular business concerned. The following exposition is bound to be somewhat generalized. Whilst the writer believes that standard costing can overcome many of the anomalies produced by an historical costing system, it is not a panacea for all ills, and where it is used without realism it can mislead as much as any other system.

Whilst much of what follows has particular reference to a manufacturing business, the general philosophy is equally applicable to other kinds of enterprise, whether they be service industries, extractive, retailing, wholesaling or even financial concerns.

Perhaps the most important, and often most neglected aspect of standard costing is that it involves a new attitude to the traditional ideas of what constitutes a unit cost, whether that cost be a particular operation in a business or a unit of output. The basic difference in attitude is that there

is no such thing as an 'actual cost'. The analysis of t
expenses of business remain largely unchanged in a standa
costing system, using the word 'expenses' to indicate ca
gories of outgoings, such as salaries, material, maintenan
and so forth. But the idea that some absolute truth is stat
when those expenses are apportioned by an exercise
arithmetic to units of output, no longer obtains if standa
costing is adopted. Ideally, basic standards are set up f
each operation and represent the amount of work that oug
to be performed in a given period. Operations in this ser
include not only jobs in the production departments b
also those necessary for the various aspects of administrati
servicing and selling. Economic prices are applied to t
various factors of production and the volume of activity
output is predicated; thus standard costs in monetary ter
are the product of price and volume. Of course, a number
reasonable assumptions must be made as to the conditio
in which the work is carried out, and one of the most impo
tant assumptions concerns the resources available for t
purpose.

Where it is desirable to record standard product costs,
the costs of services to be marketed, such figures can be bu
up by the amalgamation of the various standard job co
which are incorporated in the product. But the basic standa
is the amount of work to be carried out in performing ea
operation.

It is true that some businesses operate standard a
'actual' costing systems side by side, and compare o
with the other, no doubt creating interesting but see
ingly unproductive argument. In such cases there ari
a natural human tendency to place more credence
the so-called 'actual' cost. One reason is that the 'actu
will usually be more than the standard, leaving t
latter a suspect quantity; the other reason is that t
'actual' is the outcome of a complex and often mysterio
ritual.

Certainly a standard costing system loses much of
value if it is not used as a measure against which actual pe

ormance can be compared. But the effective comparison is
o set the actual outgoings incurred by producing a given
volume of work, or by carrying out an operation in a given
period of time, against the assessed standard cost of the
output. It is absurd to regard a substantial modern business
as spending so many pounds on producing a single product,
say, a chair or one newspaper or one tin can. Business is
concerned with expenditure on a planned volume of
materials, the running cost of machinery over a substantial
period of time, the wages cost of the personnel for the output of a production run, and the annual or even longer cost
of providing the necessary support services. Each of these
activities can be made the subject of a carefully assessed
standard or budget.

The budgetary system and the standard costing system are
interrelated. The direct material expense is likely to be
derived from an assessment of the amount of material
required for a particular job multiplied by the volume, but
the price of the material will depend on economic purchasing
contracts to meet stocking requirements.

The merits of a standard costing system may be summarized as follows:

1. Information is provided for managerial control through
   the comparison of actual expenditure against standard
   expenditure.
2. The analysis of variances between actual expenditure
   and standard expenditure saves managerial time,
   because the managers need only give their attention to
   those operations where substantial variances occur.
3. Stable and, presumably, sound figures of cost are
   provided to assist price determination.
4. Stable values are assigned to stock and work in progress, thus eliminating the anomalies described in
   preceding chapters, and assisting in the production of
   a true and fair view of profit and a reliable trend of
   profitability.

The mechanics illustrated

The process of adding values, which is inherent in an accounting system, is illustrated below in stages. The basic data are the same as were used in the illustration in Chapter 1 but a standard costing system has now replaced an historical costing system. The illustration begins when a manufacturer buys material for eventual incorporation in the production of a product.

STAGE 1. MATERIAL IS PLACED IN STOCK

	quantity	price	value
1,000 units of a certain material were purchased at a price of £1 a unit, so that the amount due to the supplier was	1,000	£1·00	£1,000
However, the standard price for this material was £0·95 a unit thus giving rise to a price variance (which was charged to a variance account) of	1,000	£0·05	£ 50
Leaving to be valued as stock in the raw material stores account	1,000	£0·95	£ 950

STAGE 2. MATERIAL IS DRAWN OUT OF STORES BY WORKSHOP

	quantity	price	value
The amount and value in stock per stage 1 was	1,000	£0·95	£ 950
800 units are withdrawn from stores by the workshop	800	£0·95	£ 760
Leaving a balance in the stock account of	200	£0·95	£ 190

But the standard quantity of material for the job was only 700 units, so that the usage variance was	100	£0·95	£ 95

STAGE 3. THE VALUE IN WORK IN PROGRESS

Deducting the above variance from the figures of the withdrawal from stock account gives the following amounts to be charged to work in progress account	700	£0·95	£ 665
Labour costs were applied to the job, the standard time and cost* being	*Hours* 180	£0·70	£ 126
Bought out components incorporated in the product were valued at	500	£0·50	£ 250
Overheads were added at the standard rate of £0·75 an hour	180	£0·75	£ 135
Giving a total value in work in progress at this point of			£1,176

	quantity	price	value
*Note on labour costs and variances			
The actual labour time and rate was	Hours 200	£0·75	£ 150
and the standard was	180	0·70	126
So that labour variances, charged to variance account, were			£ 24
The total labour variance was made up as follows:	Hours		
efficiency	20	£0·70	£ 14
rate	200	0·05	10
			£ 24

STAGE 4. THE TRANSFER TO FINISHED GOODS ACCOUNT

Two hundred units of the product have been completed in the workshop and are transferred to finished goods store. In order to ascertain the value at standard thus withdrawn from work in progress, it is necessary to calculate a standard cost per unit of product. For this purpose assume that two units of material and one of bought-out components are incorporated in each product, and that the standard labour time for completing a product is assessed at 18 minutes or 0·30 hours. The standard cost per unit of product becomes

2 units of material at £0·95	£1·900
1 unit of bought out components	0·500
0·30 hours of labour at £0·70	0·210
overheads at £0·75 per hour	0·225
	£2·835

	quantity	price	value
The value of work in progress stands at			£1,176
From this total is deducted the value at standard cost of the transfer to finished goods account, of	200	£2·835	567
Leaving a value in work in progress at standard of			£ 609

STAGE 5. DELIVERIES ARE MADE TO CUSTOMERS

	quantity	price	value
The value in the finished goods account is	200	£2·835	£ 567
Assume that half of these units are sold, the standard cost of sales being	100	£2·835	£ 284
Leaving in finished goods account	100	£2·835	£ 283

Conclusions from the illustration

The above illustration is intended to demonstrate the essentials of a system of standard costing and the manner in which it is integrated with the general accounting scheme. Only one product is envisaged in the illustration and it is obvious that considerable complexities occur where a business provides a number of products and services. Because of the immense variety of industry, large variations in procedure are met in practice, but the general philosophy of valuing only standard costs and writing off all variances from standard is common to all true systems of standard costing. The merits of the system may be summarized as follows:

1. The various stocks are valued at standard, thus providing consistency in the valuations which appear in the final accounts, and in the trend of profitability.

The cost of inefficiency in buying, labour and the utilization of overhead facilities has been eliminated from the values.

2. The use of standards for the pricing of material issues avoids the problems discussed in an earlier chapter as to whether withdrawals from stock should be priced on the basis of first-in, first-out; last-in, first-out; average cost; or any other of the innumerable conventions which are productive in stimulating academic controversy but not otherwise.

3. Many other technical problems inherent in the attempt to produce an 'actual cost' also disappear. These problems include, for instance, the question of whether to charge overtime premium in costs, whether to charge the actual cost of high-grade employees who are doing low-grade work, the question of changing overhead rates when activity changes, and so on.

4. The variances are recorded and can be advised to managers as soon as they appear, thus permitting prompt investigations and remedial action.

A comparison between the results derived from the standard costing system, as above, and the same transactions as recorded by an historical costing system, as outlined in Chapter 1, may help to underline the difference between the two approaches. The table below shows the two methods of accounting for the costs incurred during the period.

	standard costing £	historical costing £
1. COSTS APPLIED TO STOCKS		
raw material	£ 190	200
work in progress	609	850
finished goods	283	250
Total stocks	£1,082	£1,300

2. COST OF GOODS SOLD	£ 284	250

3. VARIANCES WRITTEN OFF

material price	£ 50	
material usage	95	
labour efficiency	14	
labour rate	10	
overhead (assuming actual overheads incurred of £150)	15	
Total variances	£ 184	—
Total costs incurred	£1,550	£1,550

The comparison highlights the following defects of the historical costing system:

1. The raw material stocks are inflated by the cost of inefficiencies; these costs will be set off against income when the stocks are completed and sold, thus prejudicing future profits.
2. The historical cost figure for finished goods is lower than the standard cost, because the estimate of the cost of deliveries from the shop floor was too low. One consequence is that when the production order has been completed, and all work placed in finished goods store, values not represented by tangible assets will remain in the work in progress account. These illusory values can and often do accumulate over years before the anomaly is discovered.
3. The cost of goods sold is too low in the historical costing system, again because of the error in estimating the value of deliveries from the workshop. Thus the gross profit shown on this order will be higher than it should be.

The principles of variance analysis

The foregoing exercise produced four separate variances in
direct costs, each in this case representing an apparent
inefficiency which is due for investigation by the appropriate
manager. In addition, an overhead variance was shown and
this will need special consideration. The direct cost variances
may be considered as derived from two causes:

(a) differences in price, and (b) differences in quantities,
although it is customary to give other labels to the labour
and material variances, as follows:

> Price variances $\begin{cases} \text{material price} \\ \text{labour rate} \end{cases}$

> Quantity variances $\begin{cases} \text{material usage} \\ \text{labour efficiency} \end{cases}$

The reason for the existence of these two fundamental
types of variances is that a cost is essentially the product of
multiplying a quantity by a price. Thus the amount paid to
the supplier for the material in the above illustration may
be depicted as the area of a rectangle.

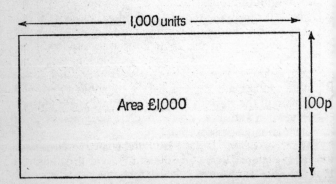

Likewise, the standard cost of this purchase may be

indicated by a rectangle, of which the side representing the price is 95p, not 100p.

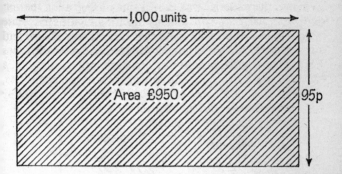

By superimposing the standard on the actual rectangle the variance appears as the area which overlaps.

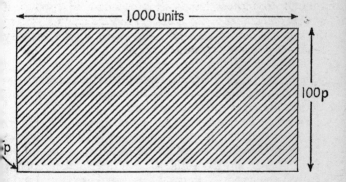

The price variance in the figure immediately above is the unshaded area of £0·05 × 1,000 = £50. It will be observed that the price variance is calculated on the actual quantity purchased, not the standard quantity. The price variance can be notified to management immediately the order for the

materials is placed, and can be recorded in the accountin
system immediately the invoice is received, thus giving som
topicality to the control mechanism.

When the material was drawn out of stores for the job
the price variance had already been eliminated from th
stock value, so that the system then needed only to deal wit
any usage variance. By superimposing a rectangle repre
senting the standard usage on a rectangle representing actua
drawings from stores, the following picture appears:

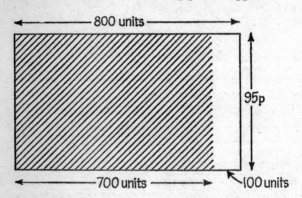

The usage variance, represented by the unshaded area, i
$100 \times £0.95 = £95$. Here it is shown that the usage varianc
is calculated by multiplying the difference in quantity by th
standard price, not the actual price.

An efficient means of ensuring that excess usage is properl
recorded is for the worshop to be issued in the first plac
only with the standard quantity of materials, the requisitio
being prepared by the works office. If this standard quantit
proves insufficient, a properly authorized excess requisitio
is presented to stores and, when valued at the standar
price, is charged to the variance account. Likewise, materia
returned to stores because it is in excess of requirement
would be recorded on a credit requisition.

The same principles apply to labour variances. The key t
the calculations is that the price variance (in the case o

labour, the hourly rate paid to the employees) applies to the actual hours spent on the job, and the quantity variance (now called 'efficiency') is costed at the standard rate.

RATE VARIANCE (DIFFERENCE IN RATES × ACTUAL HOURS)
$(£0.75 - £0.70) × 200$ $= £10$

EFFICIENCY VARIANCE (DIFFERENCE IN HOURS × STANDARD RATE)
$(200 - 180) × £0.70$ $= £14$

The control of variances

In order to simplify the exposition, the variances shown in the above illustration have all been adverse, that is, the actual expenditure exceeded the standard. Adverse variances are common occurrences, especially where the standards have been assessed on a demanding basis, but it is not unknown for favourable variances to occur. On the face of it, a favourable variance is due to efficiency above the normal; if this is the case, then there is no justification for amending the standards in an attempt to eliminate the occurrence of favourable variances in the future. Assuming that the basis on which the standards have been compiled is normally efficient operation, then a favourable variance represents exceptional efficiency or effort and should be so recorded in the accounts. Making standards more stringent might also impair their incentive effect, which is by no means an unimportant attribute to a sound standard costing system.

However, the appearance of a credit variance – and, indeed, of an exceptionally high adverse variance – may be due to an error in the assessment of the standards. In this case the variance should be clearly labelled as one awaiting revision. Revision variances are described later in this chapter.

So far as adverse variances are concerned, the fact that the actual cost exceeded the standard is not necessarily a reflection on a particular manager. Labour efficiency variances may occur not because of any fault in the efficiency of the operatives, or of their supervisors, but because, for example, they had been supplied with faulty material. A material price variance may not reflect on the buyers but may be due to a change in the specification. Overheads may be under-recovered due to restrictions on output following a fall in demand. It is likely that the ultimate responsibility for many of the variances which occur is a joint responsibility of the management team. Nevertheless, it is administratively convenient that the manager most directly concerned with the variance should bear the responsibility of explaining why it occurred and, of course, taking action to prevent it occurring in the future if it is his prime responsibility. If it is not his responsibility he will probably not be reluctant to point out who is to blame.

It is sometimes said that any variance is controllable at some level in the organization; if variances are not controllable, then the standards are due for revision. However, it is certainly true that many changes in cost are outside the power of managers to influence, especially when such changes are due to factors external to the business. The growing influence of government or government-controlled bodies can impose unavoidable price increases on industrial supplies, and price reductions on sales. Likewise wage increases are frequently the result of negotiations between unions and employers' associations and thus leave little flexibility for the individual company, except by increasing mechanization and automation. For these reasons it is desirable that in any statement of variances supplied to an individual manager, they should be separated so far as possible between those which are controllable by that manager and those which are apparently uncontrollable.

Special variances

Only the basic variances, essentially of quantity and price, have been described above. In fact, a system of variances should be constructed which caters for the needs of the management in relation to the particular circumstances of a business. Some of the more common 'special variances' are explained below.

(a) MATERIAL MIX VARIANCE

This variance can be important where there is scope for interchangeability between the various ingredients incorporated in a product. The mix variance could, for example, be important in the preparation of foodstuffs, in the manufacture of alloys and building construction materials. The following example shows the calculations involved.

Standard

Material A.	100 tons (10%) @ £3	=	£300
Material B.	400 tons (40%) @ £2	=	800
Material C.	500 tons (50%) @ £1	=	500
	1,000	*Standard cost of mix*	£1,600

Actual

Material A.	120 tons @ £3·50	=	£420
Material B.	440 tons @ £2·10	=	924
Material C.	540 tons @ £1·00	=	540
	1,100		£1,884

Three distinct variances are concealed in the above statement: price, usage and mix variances. Whilst, as shown below, the mix variance can be extracted independently of the other variances, it may assist comprehension if they are extracted in a logical order.

First reduce the actual costs to standard prices by extracting the price variance as follows:

		price variance	deduct from	leaving
Material A.	120 tons @ £3·50 — £3·00 =	£60	£420	£360
Material B.	440 tons @ £2·10 — £2·00 =	44	924	880
Material C.	540 tons @ £1·00 — £1·00 =	—	540	540
		£104	£1,884	£1,780

The difference between the values remaining and the standard must now be the usage variance, i.e., £1,780 — £1,600 = £180. Thus usage variance is made up as follows:

Material A.	120–100 tons @ £3	=	£60
Material B.	440–400 tons @ £2	=	80
Material C.	540–500 tons @ £1	=	40
			£180

The mix variance represents the extent to which the change in the proportions of the materials used has increased cost; quantities being valued at standard prices. The mix variance is, therefore, included in the above usage variance.

If the materials comprised in the actual total of 1,100 tons of product had followed the proportions shown in the standard mix, the quantities would have been as follows:

Material A.	10% of 1,100 tons	=	110 tons
Material B.	40% of 1,100 tons	=	440 tons
Material C.	50% of 1,100 tons	=	550 tons
			1,100 tons

he mix variance may now be calculated as follows:

Material	revised actual	deduct from	difference	mix variance
	110 tons	120 tons	10 @ £3	£30
	440 tons	440 tons	—	—
	550 tons	540 tons	10 @ £1	(10)
	1,100 tons	1,100 tons		£20

It may be useful to note that if the mix had been in the andard proportions, the usage variance (which may be scribed as a 'true usage variance') would have been:

Material A.	110–100 tons @ £3	=	£30
Material B.	440–400 tons @ £2	=	80
Material C.	550–500 tons @ £1	=	50
			£160

ummarizing, the total variance of £284 is made up of:

rice variance	£104
rue) usage variance	160
ix variance	20
	£284

) YIELD VARIANCE

his variance would be important in an operation where me loss in process was to be expected, but the amount of at loss needed control. Using the previous data, assume at for the standard input of 1,000 tons of material a loss `10% in weight was normal, so that the standard yield was ｀% of the input, i.e., 900 tons. Assume that the actual input

of 1,100 tons yielded 980 tons of product. The yield varian
would be calculated on the standard price of the produ
which is £$\frac{1,600}{1,000}$ = £1·6 a ton.

The standard yield from 1,100 tons @ 90%	=	990 tor
The actual yield was		980 tor
giving a yield variance of		10 tor
valued at £1·6 a ton	=	£16

Process industries produce quantitative information
yields as a matter of normal and frequently daily routi
and the actual yields are compared with norms or standar(
Whether the calculation of variances in monetary ter
would stimulate more determined action to impro
efficiency is a matter that only the managers of the busin(
concerned can decide. The belated appearance of a financ
report on a matter well known to operating manageme
does not always produce the kind of action intended.

(c) REVISION VARIANCES
These are variances which are not to be the subject
managerial action but indicate the amounts by which it
intended to revise the standards in due course. Revision
standards becomes necessary as a result of both internal a
external changes in circumstances. Internal changes m
consist of new operational methods (e.g., increased mecha1
zation), redesigning and improved specifications. Exter1
changes would embrace, for instance, wage awards a1
unavoidable price increases. It is administratively inco
venient to amend standards every time changes of this natu
occur and, in any event, too frequent revision of standar
eliminates much of the benefit of consistent accountan(
Annual revisions of standards are common practice b

me undertakings maintain standards for a number of
ars.

) CALENDAR VARIANCES

alendar variances are sometimes extracted to cover over-
ad costs incurred during public holidays and other non-
orking days, where these vacations were not accounted for
the original standards.

) IDLE TIME VARIANCES

hese are normally calculations at standard rates of the cost
various categories of idle time, including waiting for work
materials, sickness, attending meetings, machine break-
wn, power failure, etc.

verhead variances

he calculation of overhead variances takes a somewhat
fferent form from that applied to direct cost variances,
rgely because with direct cost variances only one kind of
pense is involved, i.e., material or labour, whereas over-
ads consist of an amalgamation of many different kinds of
pense. The basic division between price and quantity
riances applies to overhead variances but it is often
plicit rather than explicit in the figures. Thus, for example,
though it would be possible to express one part of the
ephone bill as representing so many calls at a certain
ice, this approach could not be applied so easily to the
ntal. The other characteristic of overheads which distin-
ishes them from direct costs is that a large proportion of
erheads do not move in the short term in relation to
tivity; and it is the short term with which we are largely
ncerned for control purposes.

On the basis, however, that the overhead expenses repre-
nt the cost of facilities brought into being to service and
stain the output of the business, then it would be useful to
easure the extent to which they are greater or less than are
quired for that purpose. In other words, to what extent

does the business contain idle facilities or incur inappropriat
expenses?

To summarize the argument at this point, it appears tha
the basic information required by management with respec
to overheads is as follows:

1. Is the cost of overheads greater or less than it shoul
   be? Probably the most acceptable way of presentin
   the answer to this question would be by comparin
   actual costs against a carefully assessed budget o
   standard.
2. To what extent do the overhead expenses of the busines
   represent idle facilities? Facilities will tend to be idle i
   the business is not working to a reasonable level c
   capacity. Facilities will be wasted if they have to b
   applied to sustaining inefficient performance.

In constructing a system of information to managemen
designed to indicate answers to these questions the essentia
needs will be (a) to prepare budgets of overheads; (b) t
assess a reasonable level of capacity working for the busi
ness; and (c) to organize a system for recording actua
expenses and actual activity, the latter also involving stati
tics as to efficiency. From (a) and (b) the standard overhea
rate will be calculated; ideally separate standard rates shoul
be calculated for each major centre of activity. As discusse
earlier, the activity of a business or of a workshop in
business cannot always be effectively measured by simpl
counting units or weight of output, particularly where tha
output contains many different products or kinds of produc
in varying proportions. Some factor representing the tim
involved in the production is usually considered to be
sound overall measure of activity and, in consequence, c
forming a base for the overhead rate.

It is the standard rate, not an actual rate, which will b
applied to cost units for the purpose of valuing work i
progress and, eventually, finished goods stock.

If the standard rate is to be applied to some measure c

me, say man hours or machine hours, then that rate must
e applied to the standard times required for each job or
peration, not the hours actually spent on the jobs. In this
ay, the work will be valued at standard cost, so far as its
verhead content is concerned, and the result will be that the
tandard cost will be set against sales of the goods in order
) derive the gross profit on sales. Any balance of overheads
ver-recovered or under-recovered will be written off in the
rofit and loss account as a credit or debit and represents
le cost of inefficiency or of idle resources. With a
tandard costing system the objective is not to arrive at a
ate which will necessarily absorb all the overheads but
) value the work on the basis of reasonably efficient
perations.

It follows that the standard rate must be based on a
easonable level of capacity utilization; if the system is to
ct as an incentive, the level of utilization should be that
'hich is attainable in normal conditions – under exceptional
ressure it may at times even be exceeded. It will be observed
lat the expected level of sales, or the output actually planned
or a period, is irrelevant in the establishment of the over-
ead rate. Demand will presumably have been taken into
ccount in setting up an operation at a certain level of
apacity.

In the case of many items of overhead expense it should
e possible to make an objective assessment of the resources
equired to sustain capacity working. Those items of over-
ead, such as consumable stores, power, and much of the
idirect labour should in the short term (with which we are
rimarily concerned) move in direct ratio to output and,
fter a period of experience, the budgeted expenditure can
e assessed on this basis. By and large the non-variable ex-
enses will require individual assessment, preferably with
he aid of work study and systems analysis; but even the
udgets of non-variable overheads should have regard to
'hat is required to service the output over the long term.
Much will depend on the wit and experience of the managers
nd accountants concerned in the exercise, and it is

sometimes curious how trial and error produce the answe
quicker than science. Although frequent changes in th
overhead rate are confusing, it is not suggested that such
rate be fixed for all time. The budgets and standards will be
refined from time to time; the capacity of the business ma
be increased by developments in technology or additions t
resources; external influences, such as general price change
will affect the budgets.

Once the budgets and standards have been established,
is usually considered sufficient for variances to be extracte
and advised to the managers concerned at monthly interval
For this purpose the accounting system must be organize
to produce the results promptly after the end of each mont
This will involve some estimation in the assessment of actu
overhead costs. The variances will, however, never be
absolutely accurate but merely represent signposts fe
managerial investigation and action. In this ligh
prompt reporting of results containing some element
approximation is far more effective than more accura
figures which are advised so late that they have becon
merely history.

Because the variable overheads should move in relatic
to the output produced, whilst the remaining overheads w
be largely independent of that output, it will be desirable
treat each category of expense separately. In the examp
set out below it is assumed that various kinds and measur
ments of product are produced and that the key factor fe
all products is standard hours. Assume also that the peric
concerned is one month.

1. BUDGETS
   (*a*) *Output* (This represents a reasonable level
   of capacity working, expressed in terms of
   the key factor.)   5,000 hou
   (*b*) *Variable overheads*   £15,000
   (*c*) *Non-variable overheads*   £10,000

STANDARD OVERHEAD RATES

Derived from the above figures, these are:

(i) Variable overheads: £$\dfrac{15,000}{5,000}$ = £3 an hour

(ii) Non-variable overheads: £$\dfrac{10,000}{5,000}$ = £2 an hour

ACTUAL RESULTS

(a) *Output* (This is the standard hours assessed for all the jobs undertaken during the period)	4,500 standard hours
(b) *Actual time worked*	4,800 hours
(c) *Actual variable overheads*	£14,000
(d) *Actual non-variable overheads*	£11,500
(e) *Overheads applied to work in progress*	
(i) *variable:* @ £3 an hour	£13,500
(ii) *non-variable:* @ £2 an hour	9,000
total 'recovery'	£22,500

There is a real practical difficulty in ascertaining the standard hours of the actual work done in such a short period as a month because some of the jobs will have been started in the previous months and some will be still in progress at the end of the month. Where the jobs are of short duration, e.g., lasting for no more than a few days in each case, it may be sufficiently accurate to use the standard times of only the jobs completed in each period. In other cases, estimates will have to be made of the degree of completion of each job, and the standard time allowed for the whole job apportioned accordingly.

4. VARIABLE OVERHEAD VARIANCES

  (*a*) *Budget variance*

Budget	£15,000
Actual	14,000

    variance   £1,000 favourable

Note: This variance, which customarily appears on cost and budget comparison statements, is quite misleading. The budget was established in order to calculate the overhead rate; in this case it serves no other purpose because the allowable expenditure is dependent on the output which is achieved. The following variance is more informative.

  (*b*) *Expenditure variance*
    standard expenditure:

£3 × 4,500 hours	£13,500
actual expenditure	14,000

    variance   £500 adverse

The indications from this variance are that there has been overspending amongst the variable overheads, not under spending, as might have been inferred from 4 (*a*) above. Note that the standard is the standard rate applied to the standard hours, not to the actual hours worked. If the rate had been applied to the actual hours, i.e., £3 × 4,800 = £14,400, it would have appeared that there had been an under-spending of £400, and the value charged to work in progress would have been £900 more than it would have been had the standard hours been used. However, the presumption is that the 300 hours taken on the work above standard was due to inefficiency and should not be taken to justify increased spending on overheads above standard. Nor should inefficiency have the effect of increasing work in progress and stock values.

5. NON-VARIABLE OVERHEAD VARIANCES

(a) *Budget variance*

Budget	£10,000
actual expenditure	11,500
variance	£1,500 adverse

As compared with the budget variance for variable expenditure, the above figure does suggest that there has been an overspending amongst the items making up the non-variable overheads, because the budget is based on the assumption that the expenditure is unrelated to output in the short term. This variance does, however, need interpreting with care, for if output remains for many months below attainable capacity working, the management would undoubtedly require these overheads to be reduced below the amount necessary for capacity working. Likewise, if output above normal utilization of capacity was maintained for a considerable number of months, some overspending above the budget might be justifiable. In the present example, activity is below capacity and, consequently, the overspending would merit careful investigation.

(b) *Volume variance*

The volume of output, in terms of standard hours is 5,000 − 4,500 = 500 less than it could have been. This statement may be easier to comprehend if the business was producing a uniform product and units of product were substituted for hours. Valued at the standard rate of £2 an hour this means that the business incurred £1,000 in non-variable overheads which could not be applied to product; in other words this was wasted expense. Alternatively, the volume variance may be expressed as:

Budget	£10,000
Standard cost of actual output:	

£2 × 4,500 std. hours	9,000
variance	£1,000 adverse

This variance may, however, be subdivided because it consists of (a) inefficiency, by reason of the fact that only 4,500 standard hours of work (or 4,500 units of product) were produced by the expenditure of 4,800 actual hours; and (b) under-utilization as a result of the 200 hours which could have been generated.

(c) *Efficiency variance*
  4,500 − 4,800 = 300 hours @ £2 = £ 600 adverse
(d) *Utilization of capacity variance*
  5,000 − 4,800 = 200 hours @ £2 = £ 400 adverse

  total, as volume variance   £1,000 adverse

Finally, it may be worth emphasizing the danger of the foregoing arithmetic being accepted as the ultimate truth. Variances are nothing more than warning signs which merit investigation. This is particularly true of overhead variances because many expenses of this nature result from policy decisions in respect of the future. An increasing proportion of current business outgoings has no relevance to current production but is designed to meet anticipated needs of perhaps, many years hence. Examples are training and management development schemes, the installation of systems and all kinds of research.

6   The Use and Abuse of Marginal Costing

Introductory: definitions, importance for decision-making, short term or long term; Marginal costing and forward planning; Example of planning with marginal costs; Marginal costs and the product mix; Marginal costs and break-even levels; Marginal costs and pricing – a case study; Other applications: make or buy decisions, alternative methods of production, projects of capital investment

Introductory

In a previous chapter, the marginal cost was defined as the change in total costs which was brought about by increasing or decreasing output by a specified quantity. Managers are more likely to be interested in an increase rather than a decrease in output and in this context an alternative definition of marginal cost is the additional outgoings caused by additional production.

Because marginal cost is concerned only with outgoings, that is, money to be spent in the period concerned, two kinds of cost normally incorporated in average or conventional cost figures are excluded. The categories of expenses which do not form part of the marginal cost are: (a) deferred charges or 'sunk costs' such as depreciation, which represents the carrying forward of part of an expenditure of a past period; and (b) expenses which would continue whether or not the change in output was affected, of which typical examples are rent of the business premises and much of the administrative cost of managing a business, as such.

Marginal costing, or variants thereof, is also known by other titles, such as differential costing, variable costing and direct costing. Differential costing specifically refers to different levels of output; variable costing is often treated as synonymous with marginal costing because the expenses which vary in relation to output will necessarily be of a marginal nature; direct costs are usually wholly variable, although some variable expenses (paint is a good example) are excluded from direct costing on grounds of impractica bility. On the assumption that the fixed or non-variable expenses are in fact fixed and immutable, they are excluded from the marginal cost. However, in the long run, and with a sufficient change in the volume of output, those expenses which a business has hitherto regarded as fixed will become at least in part, variable and to that extent marginal.

The importance of marginal costing in connection with management decisions is that those decisions are essentially concerned with the future, and marginal costing refers to future income and future outgoings. It is said that money which is already spent, such as on the purchase of a machine or a project of research and development, has no relevance to management decision-making which is concerned with money to be spent and income to be received. The past is history and its only value is that it may be a guide to the future, albeit sometimes a misleading one. This view of the exclusive relevance of future outgoings to management decisions needs to be qualified by the fact that money invested in the past in, for instance, machinery, research and perhaps publicity, has usually acquired an asset which is of current value to the business, although it may have little value as a saleable item. If the future production and sale of a product depends on the use of existing plant or other assets paid for some time ago, there is often a presumption that those assets could have been applied to some other productive purpose. To the extent that this is so, the existence of the assets is relevant to decisions about the future and their value to the business is also relevant as an opportunity cost. Furthermore, if the product concerned is likely o endure, the income derivable from it must be sufficient o replace the asset on which its survival depends. The cost of replacement is a future outgoing and hence a marginal cost.

It is customary to refer to marginal costing as short-term costing and sometimes as 'crisis costing', but the period covered by the short term in this context is rarely defined, except perhaps by the meaningless phrase that 'it depends on circumstances'. Of course it does! But what are the circumstances on which it depends? If the idea of variable costing is substituted for marginal costing, then the reference is understandable because the short term becomes the period within which no change occurs in the so-called fixed costs. If, however, one takes the wider view that the marginal cost covers the change in *total* expenses resulting from changes in activity, then there seems to be no logical reason why some arbitrary time limit should be attributed to the true marginal cost. This reflection may be considered as particularly apposite in an age when external pressures force many business undertakings to carry out exercises of long term planning.

Marginal costing and forward planning

The above introduction suggests that the idea of the marginal cost is not without its complexities. One of the practical difficulties in a given situation is to quantify the marginal cost and, indeed, the marginal income. As a rough practical guide it is customary to treat the variable costs as equivalent to marginal costs although, as suggested above, this will be an essentially short-term viewpoint. Assume that a reasonable approximation of both variable and non-variable costs can be made. Proceeding on the basis that the *rate* of variable costs will remain static in relation to production, and that the fixed or non-variable costs will not alter, it will be possible to construct a simple, rough and ready, but useful, guide to future profitability.

Instead of preparing a profit and loss account forecast in

the traditional style, the account may be prepared on the following lines:

Sales	£150,000
Variable costs	120,000
Contribution	£ 30,000
Fixed expense	15,000
Profit	£ 15,000

Explanatory notes:

1. The variable costs are quite different from the cost of goods sold deducted from sales in the conventional profit and loss account in order to arrive at the gross profit. In the conventional statement the cost of goods sold will consist of the direct cost of the products sold. This direct cost will be composed of the production-variable costs of labour and material, but to those costs there will be added an overhead rate which will represent both variable and non-variable production expenses relevant to the product. In the marginal form of statement the variable expenses deducted from sales are variable expenses incurred in the sales and administrative departments as well as in the production department.

2. The figure of Contribution indicates the extent to which the sales, less variable expenses, contribute towards the fixed expenses and the profit of the business. A statement of this nature prepared under product lines would show the various contributions made by each line to meeting the fixed overheads of the business and to overall profit. A statement of this nature is shown later in this chapter.

3. The fixed or non-variable expenses plus the required profit represent the sum which must be met by the contributions from the various product lines. In the following calculations, fixed expenses are assumed to remain un-

altered by changes in activity, but this will be only true in the short term, i.e., until the facilities involved can be applied elsewhere or disposed of. In this simple form of statement the fixed expense total is likely to include a number of items of semi-variable expenses, but this complication is also ignored in the calculations.

This elemental form of marginal costing statement can now be used to make some useful assessments of (a) the effect on profit of altering sales volume; (b) the break-even point of the business in terms of sales; and (c) the value of sales required to produce a given profit (possibly calculated as a percentage return on capital employed in the business). In all the following calculations the price of the sales is assumed to remain unaltered; the variable costs remain at a fixed percentage to sales, i.e., 80%; and the fixed expenses remain unaltered in total.

1. If it is anticipated that sales will fall to £100,000, the resulting profit is calculated as follows:

The contribution is 20% of sales and the amount of the contribution equals fixed expenses plus the profit. The only unknown is the profit.

Then, 20% of £100,000	=	£15,000 + profit
Profit	=	£ 5,000

The statement can now be redrafted to show the expected position.

Sales	£100,000
variable costs 80%	80,000
Contribution	£ 20,000
fixed expense	15,000
Profit	£ 5,000

2. The break-even point is where profit is nil, and the unknown in this case is the sales value.

$$
\begin{aligned}
\text{Then, Sales} - 80\% \text{ of sales} &= £15,000 + 0 \\
20\% \text{ of sales} &= £15,000 \\
\text{Sales} &= £75,000
\end{aligned}
$$

3. If the required profit is £25,000 and the value of sales turnover is required, the calculation is as follows:

$$
\begin{aligned}
\text{Sales} - 80\% \text{ of sales} &= £15,000 + £25,000 \\
20\% \text{ of sales} &= £40,000 \\
\text{Sales} &= £200,000
\end{aligned}
$$

The reader may be interested in redrafting the marginal cost statement in the case of examples (2) and (3).

A more complex example

It will be recognized that the preceding examples are much too simple to be used for more than 'off the cuff' forecasts and in reality many complications will be present in any attempt to forecast business profits. The complications will, for example, include the fact that sales will be made at different prices to different segments of the market; variable costs will change in rate per unit, due, amongst other factors, to external price changes; non-variable costs will not in fact remain static; and the required profit will be a function of the capital employed, which is itself variable. All these and other changing factors can, however, be introduced into the model, although in a large business the use of a computer or of a computer service bureau may become necessary. An indication of how various changing factors can be brought into the exercise are shown by the following further example.

Assume that the marginal cost statement drawn up for a venture in its first year of operation is as follows:

Sales:	Total	Per Unit
50,000 units at a price of £1·7 a unit	£85,000	£1·70
Variable costs	50,000	1·00
Contribution	£35,000	£0·70
Fixed costs	60,000	1·20
Loss	£25,000	£0·50

Plans are in course of preparation for a very large increase in output and sales in the following year and the following matters are to be taken into account:

1. The Sales Department say that they can sell up to 80,000 units of the product in the present market at the existing price of £1·7 but additional sales can only be made in special markets (Note: this could mean overseas markets) where the price would have to fall to £1·5 a unit.
2. Because of an impending wage award and other increases in external prices variable costs are likely to rise by 10%.
3. In order to cope with output above the present levels an additional £10,000 must be added to what have hitherto been regarded as fixed costs.
4. The management require a profit target of 10% on capital employed. The turnover rate of capital employed in terms of sales value is likely to be 2, i.e., sales will be twice capital employed.

Note: The exercise still contains a feature that would be quite unreal in many businesses in that the above sales apparently represent completely uniform production. However, it would not be difficult to represent the sales as composed of a number of different units at various prices.

Another alternative is to assume that the units are units of the key factor used to produce all the different types of product, typical key factors being, for example, man hours, machine hours; or whatever unit is universal to all product manufacture. This solution also assumes that pricing is based on remuneration for use of the key factor in the business – by no means an illogical assumption.

The main purpose is to determine what volume of sales is required to produce the target profit. It is obvious from inspection that the sales must exceed 80,000 units, whereafter price will fall to £1·5 a unit. The procedure is to substitute figures for the following expression:

Sales – variable costs = fixed costs + profit

The unknown, represented in the following calculation by X, is the sales in units above 80,000. On this basis the various factors in the equation may be detailed.

Sales are: £1·7 × 80,000 + £1·5X = £136,000 + £1·5X
Variable costs are: £1·1 (80,000 + X) = £88,000 + X
Fixed costs are: £60,000 + 10,000 = £70,000
Profit is: 10% of $\dfrac{\text{sales}}{2} = \dfrac{£136,000 + £1·5X}{20}$

The equation now becomes:
(£136,000 + £1·5X) − (£88,000 + X) = £70,000 + $\dfrac{£136,000 + £1·5X}{20}$

It will be found from this equation that X = 88,692

The future plan may now be shown as a marginal cost statement as follows:

Sales:		*in thousands*
	80,000 @ £1·7	£136·0
	88,692 @ £1·5	133·0
	168,692	£269·0

Variable costs:	
168,692 @ £1·1	185·5
Contribution	£ 83·5
Fixed costs	70·0
Profit	£ 13·5

Check: 10% of $\dfrac{£269\cdot0}{2}$ $=$ £ 13·5

Marginal costs and the product mix

So far the exercises have illustrated the use of the marginal costing idea in relation to the company or production unit as a whole. One important responsibility of management is to ensure that the resources of the business are applied in the most profitable manner for the purpose of achieving the overall plan. This means, in effect, for the business to concentrate on the most profitable products within the limitations imposed. An overall limitation on any business operations is the supply of funds but, with the use of temporary borrowings and other devices, the financial limitation is, at least with the larger business, one of considerable flexibility. Another major limitation is the market for a particular class of goods or services, but here again the efforts of the marketing function can usually provide some flexibility through advertising, discounts and sales effort in general. One limitation which is not always so amenable to expansion is the capacity of the plant to produce the goods. There will usually be a number of factors which impose a limit to the output but there will be one factor which is predominant, and which is here called the key limiting factor. This factor will vary with circumstances but may be the supply of skilled operatives represented by the man hours which can be generated, the capacity of key machines, the supply of vital materials and the space available.

Where a business produces a variety of goods or services,

each making varying use of the key limiting factors in the business, the objective should be to sell a sales mix which gives the optimum profit per unit of the limiting factor. In other words effort should be applied in priority to those products which show a greatest surplus in these terms but, of course, the market will restrict the amount which can be sold of any particular line.

In calculating the profit per unit of the limiting factor, and subject to the qualifications indicated in the first part of this chapter, the cost to be deducted from the sales of the product should be the marginal cost. Fixed costs, which will continue whether a particular product is sold or not, and sunk costs representing money already spent, should both be ignored for the purpose.

This important application of marginal costs is illustrated by the following example. For clarity only two products have been shown, but they may be taken to represent a range of products. The limiting factor is assumed to be the number of man hours which can be generated in the business and this is estimated at 100,000 in a given period. The fixed costs are not allocated or apportioned to the respective products on the grounds that they consist of common services which are incapable of being attributed to each product except on an arbitrary basis.

The present situation is shown by the following statement:

	Product A	Product B	Total
(a) PRESENT POSITION			
units produced	20,000	40,000	
hours per unit	1	2	
total hours	20,000	80,000	100,000
price per unit	£2	£0·5	
Sales	£40,000	£20,000	£60,000
% age contribution on sales	10%	60%	
Contribution	£ 4,000	£12,000	£16,000
Fixed costs			18,000
Loss			£2,000

The problem is to eliminate the loss and to substitute a profit. To what extent can this be achieved by altering the product mix, that is by producing and selling with a different relationship between the products? Superficially it would appear that since product B makes a contribution of 60% on sales compared with the mere 10% for product A, resources should be concentrated on product B. Consider, therefore, the result of applying all the hours available to product B.

hours	100,000
hours per unit	2
units	50,000
price per unit	£ 0·5
Sales	£25,000
Contribution @ 60%	15,000
Fixed costs	18,000
Loss	£ 3,000

The loss is now greater than before, suggesting that percentages on sales can be quite misleading as a guide to the most profitable allocation of the resources of a business.

What is the position when all the hours are applied to the apparently least profitable product, A?

hours	100,000
hours per unit	1
units	100,000
price per unit	£2
Sales	£200,000
Contribution, 10%	£20,000
Fixed cost	18,000
Profit	£ 2,000

Now the original loss of £2,000 has been converted into a profit of £2,000. The reason is that the contribution per unit of the limiting factor, in this case hours, is greatest in the case of product A.

		per hour		
		A		B
price		£2·00		£0·25
variable cost	$\frac{36}{20}$	1·80	$\frac{8}{80}$	0·10
contribution		£0·20		£0·15

It is thus the last piece of arithmetic, above, which will determine the priorities to be accorded to the various products. Obviously, the next consideration is the amount of the potential sales of each product, but the business should aim to obtain the greatest sales of those products which will produce the greatest contribution per unit of the limiting factor. Having disposed of the key limiting factor so far as output is concerned, and the limitation of the potential sales, it may be found that a further limiting factor, say, material supplies, enters into the picture, and so on.

It may be that the potential market is so large that it does not present an effective limitation to the output to be produced. In this case, the objective of the business, subject to policy considerations, will be to expand the limiting factors as far as possible so that the utmost sales can be made of the most profitable products in the sense indicated above.

One further point of interest in connection with this topic is the use of marginal costs (represented in this case by variable costs) and the contribution to determine the profitability of the products. Given the assumption that the fixed costs will continue at the same level whatever the relationship between the output of the products, then those costs are irrelevant to the exercise. In fact, any attempt to apportion such costs to the various products in an arbitrary manner will simply produce misleading figures. Thus, if the allocation is made on the basis of sales turnover, as is quite customary, the result will be as follows, using the original statement for the purpose:

APPORTIONING FIXED COSTS ON SALES TURNOVER

	A	B	Total
Contribution	£ 4,000	£12,000	£16,000
Fixed costs			
proportion	2/3rds	1/3rd	
apportionment	£12,000	£ 6,000	£18,000
		profit	(loss)
(loss)	£(8,000)	£ 6,000	£ 2,000

This apportionment will tend to emphasize the false impression of A being a loss-maker. However, having decided that the truth lies in the reverse proposition, the management should next consider whether concentration on A would affect the fixed facilities required to serve the business. If, for instance, A was an exceptionally bulky article, an increase in the production of this product might require the introduction of more space and more handling staff, thus increasing the fixed costs, and that increase would be a relevant cost so far as A was concerned. It would also be a marginal cost. Alternatively, increased production of A might leave some of the fixed facilities redundant to requirements. Assuming that they could be used in some other profitable activity, and only on this assumption, a concentration on A would to this extent bring further profit into the business, and this factor in the situation would also be relevant.

Marginal costs and break-even levels

The break-even level is that at which sales just cover fixed expenses and variable expenses. It is usually desirable for the management team to be aware of the break-even point, particularly in the case of a new venture because this shows the minimum level at which activity must be held. In calculating the break-even level for the information of management it is desirable that a minimum profit be included in costs and this minimum should be calculated as a basic return on capital employed. It is a debatable point whether the basic return on capital should be treated as a variable or a fixed cost; usually the latter, although in fact the capital employed in a particular venture is bound to alter in relation to activity. Perhaps the answer is to treat this minimum return as a completely separate item from other costs.

The break-even level can be calculated in the manner shown earlier in this chapter or may be shown by a graph of which two examples follow. The first is based on the original figures of the last example, that is before taking into account the increase of £10,000 in fixed expenses, the rise to £1·1 in variable expenses and the change in the sales price. At the break-even level the contribution will equal the fixed costs and the rate of contribution is £0·7 per unit, so that the calculation is:

$$\frac{£60,000}{0·7} = 85,700 \text{ units approx}$$

The second example shows the effect on the break-even point of the various changes which have occurred in price and costs, and it will be observed that this has caused a dramatic rise in that point from an output of 85,700 units to an output of 135,000 units, i.e., nearly 60%. This is due to the fact that a large increase in sales is required to cover the £10,000 rise in fixed expenses, added to which the margin between the price and the variable cost has fallen.

BREAK-EVEN CHART 1

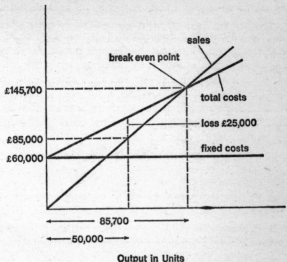

It is not an uncommon occurrence in a competitive business to find that the margin between price and variable cost
is small so that any increase in fixed expenses causes a sharp
rise in the amount of output required to reach the break-even
point. A business with a high break-even point is vulnerable
to recessions in trade and those concerns with a heavy
investment in machinery and automation are always under
pressure to maintain turnover. The device of maintaining
turnover by marginal pricing is discussed in the next section.

Marginal costs and pricing

The use of marginal pricing for particular purposes is a well-
known business stratagem. A marginal price is commonly
understood to mean one which is below full cost; full cost

meaning direct cost plus a 'fair share' of all the overheads
the business. Pricing on a marginal basis is often considere
in business to be a highly dangerous procedure to be used on
in exceptional situations. It is regarded as dangerous be
cause: (a) marginal pricing in a segment of the market ca
lead to an enforced reduction of prices in other segment
and (b) if too many products were priced on a margina
basis the contributions they make might be insufficient t
produce a reasonable profit or, in the extreme, to meet th
fixed expenses of the business. Other authorities maintai
that, to the extent that costs influence price, the costs con
cerned must always be the marginal costs. It is a matter

BREAK-EVEN CHART 2

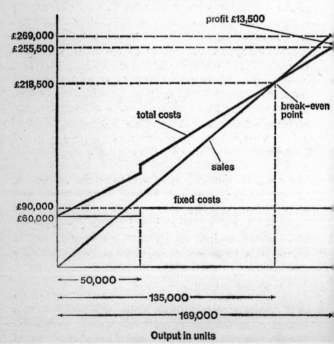

budgeting to ensure that the required contribution is realized. These commonly expressed ideas no doubt reflect the results of experience and, in consequence, are likely to contain a substantial element of truth. Nevertheless, the frequent assertion that marginal pricing is a dangerous device justifies further examination of the subject.

The principles which, it is suggested, should apply to the use of costs in pricing a product are set out below and generally derive from the various discussions in this book related to the nature of costs.

1. The economist's theoretical principle to the effect that profit is maximized where marginal cost equals marginal revenue needs to be borne in mind. This means in effect that it remains worthwhile for a business to continue to increase output and sales, even though the difference between marginal costs and additional sales is diminishing, because whilst there remains a surplus each additional sale will add to profit. The assumption is that the difference between marginal cost and marginal sales will diminish as output is expanded because price may have to be reduced to obtain the additional sales and at the same time marginal cost may rise due to the pressure on the resources of the business.

2. The essential question is to maximize the product of net income and volume of output; net income in this sense meaning sales less marginal costs. Since, however, increased output will need to be financed, the marginal costs should include an element for interest on the capital to be employed at the appropriate level of output.

3. There will normally be a range of price levels acceptable in a particular market at a given point of time and, assuming the market is sensitive to price, the volume of sales is likely to depend on the price at which the

goods are to be put on the market.

4. Where, as is frequently the case, a range of products is offered by a business unit, effort should be directed towards selling those products which produce the largest surplus per unit of the limiting factor.

5. In considering the marginal cost for the purpose it is necessary to bear in mind that: (a) increased output is likely in the long term to cause an increase in what have hitherto been regarded as the fixed costs of the business and (b) the cost of unused facilities is not a cost which is relevant to a product nor, indeed, to the pricing exercise at all, except where additional output uses those facilities.

In order to illustrate the foregoing points in a more or less practical form, the following case study is submitted for consideration. The reader will appreciate that to clarify the exposition, the case study attempts to concentrate on the essentials and thus ignores a large number of complexities which would be present in a real situation.

Case Margins

The capital employed of a company is £100,000, all represented by ordinary shares. It makes a standard product which it sells in UK markets only. At the best price it can get in the market, which is approximately equal to total costs, the sales department is unable to sell more than 50% of the capacity, which is 200,000 units of the product. The accountant summarizes the position in what he calls 'marginal form' as follows:

in thousands per unit

Sales			
units		100·0	
		——	
value		£200·0	£2·00
Less: variable costs:			
production	£70·0		
selling & admin	30·0		
	——		
		100·0	1·00
		——	——
Contribution		£100·0	£1·00
Less: fixed costs:			
production	£55·0		
selling & admin	45·0		
	——		
		100·0	1·00
		——	——
Profit		£ —	£ —
		══	══

With a view to increasing output, the Managing Director
instructs the sales department to seek outlets abroad.
Eventually the Sales Manager produces a draft contract
with Polski SA which will absorb a further 10% of the
capacity, i.e., 20,000 units, but the best price he can obtain
for this contract is only £1·5 a unit, which he admits is below
total costs. The Accountant, however, maintains that this
contract would add £10,000 to profits, assuming no further
fixed costs were incurred. He demonstrates this assertion
with the following statement:

	present position	*in thousands* Polski contract	Totals
Sales			
units	100·0	20·0	120·0
price (in unit £s)	£ 2·0	£ 1·5	
value	£200·0	£30·0	£230·0
Less: variable costs @ £1	100·0	20·0	120·0
Contribution	£100·0	£10·0	£110·0
Fixed costs			100·0
Profit			£ 10·0

On this basis the contract is accepted and the company duly
makes nearly £10,000 profit in the year, a small shortfall
being due to a rise in administrative expenses.

Next year the Sales Manager reports with some satis-
faction that he has now negotiated contracts abroad at a
price of £1·5, and these contracts, together with the Polski
contract, will absorb 50% of the capacity, so that the company will be fully employed. The Accountant thereupon
draws up another statement showing that as a result of the
Sales Manager's action profit will rise to £50,000.

	U.K.	*in thousands* overseas	total
Sales			
units	100·0	100·0	200·0
price	£ 2·0	£ 1·5	
value	£200·0	£150·0	£350·0
Less: variable costs @ £1	100·0	100·0	200·0
Contribution	£100·0	£ 50·0	£150·0
Fixed costs			100·0
Profit			£ 50·0

The Managing Director is heard to say that he cannot understand how they have begun to make profits by selling at below costs, but he agrees to the proposals and is somewhat surprised to find that in fact the profit for the year is not far short of the £50,000 predicted by the Accountant, although administrative expenses showed a further rise and interest on borrowings of £30,000 to finance the development absorbed £3,000 of the profit.

The management becomes very worried when at the end of the year the product appears in the UK market at a price of £1·75 a unit. Accordingly the company's UK price is reduced to this figure, with a consequent fall in profitability, but demand continues strong from overseas at the price of £1·5 and could easily absorb the whole of the company's output. The Sales Manager loses no time in informing the Production Manager that he could now buy the product from other suppliers at below the company's costs and relations between the two become strained. Eventually they agree to blame the Accountant.

The Managing Director thereupon calls a meeting for which the agenda contained the following two items only:

1. What is the cost of the product?
2. What is the correct basis for determining our price?

COMMENTS ON THE CASE

1. The case sets out the elements of a fairly common situation where a business is not selling and therefore not producing the volume of output which it has been set up to produce. There may be many reasons for this situation, beginning with the fact that the market concerned has limited potential, but also lack of adequate sales effort or acceptable product and a price which is uncompetitive. In this particular case the decision is taken to increase turnover by extending into a fresh market overseas.

2. So far as the existing position is concerned, there is an implication that the company has not considered the

maximization of profit through the optimum balance of price volume and costs, this being inferred from the fact that we are told it is selling 'at the best price it can get in the market'. The best price may not be the most remunerative price.

3.   However, the attempt to remedy the situation which is adopted, that of accepting a contract for 20,000 units with Polski SA, is undoubtedly sound as a short-term measure for it does increase profits by £10,000 subject to the increase in administrative expenses. The reason, of course, is that although this contract is priced below total cost of £2 a unit, it is above the apparent marginal cost of £1 a unit. Nevertheless, it is noted that a small rise occurs in administrative expenses, indicating that the cost of additional output is rarely confined to variable cost but also affects to some degree what had hitherto been regarded as a fixed cost.

4.   For similar reasons the subsequent acceptance of further overseas contracts at below total cost to the extent of half the capacity also increases profit, but it is to be observed that the true marginal cost of the additional orders now includes not only a further increase in administrative expenses but also the cost of borrowings to finance the rise in turnover. This finance is specifically required to provide funds for the inevitable further investment in receivables and stock as well as additional ready cash.

5.   Subsequently, the same product appears on the UK market at below the company's price of £2 and below its former total cost. This could have been due to resales by overseas buyers, thus indicating one of the dangers of marginal pricing in what are thought to be special markets. Alternatively, it could have been due merely to an attempt by competitors in the UK to obtain larger turnover by reducing their prices and obtaining part of the market share of the company under consideration.

6.   The Managing Director asks the direct question: What is the cost of the product? This question implies that he is under the illusion that cost in his business is an absolute and unalterable fact. He should be informed that cost depends:

) on the purpose for which it is required; and (b) the circumstances in which it is to be used. In this case the purpose for which it is required is to assist in price determination. In particular it is required for the purpose of indicating the minimum price at which additional sales may be made to help in absorbing spare capacity. As shown by this case the price, or at least the acceptable price range, tends to be dictated by the market; the minimum cost, subject to the qualification mentioned below, is the marginal cost.

7. The circumstances to be taken into account when calculating a cost for the purposes in mind include the question as to whether the cost is to be considered of a short-term or long-term nature. The answer to that question in turn depends on whether the pricing exercise is to be regarded merely as a temporary expedient to raise turnover until the basic markets can be developed to absorb capacity, or whether the new markets will constitute a permanent feature of the sales outlets of the business. If the exercise is intended as short term or temporary only, then the minimum cost for the purpose is the variable cost of £1 plus additions to be assessed for any increase in 'fixed costs' (such as additional administrative expenses) which will be incurred. In addition, further interest on capital must be taken into account where the rise in turnover creates a need for more funds.

8. If the exercise is intended as a long-term situation where half the capacity will be sold to UK markets and half to overseas markets, then the relevant costs are not confined to the variable costs. There is a presumption that, subject to detailed investigation, half the facilities represented by the fixed overheads are used by each of these two main markets. If this were not so each half of those expenses could, presumably, be avoided or the facilities they represent applied to some other remunerative purpose. This being so, the long-term position can be indicated by the following statement:

	in thousands		
	UK	*overseas*	*total*
Contribution	£100·0	£50·0	£150·0
Less: Fixed costs apportioned equally to each market	50·0	50·0	100·0
Profit	£ 50·0	—	£ 50·0

9. The apportionment of the fixed expenses above
clearly approximate. A more accurate picture would
obtained by making an assessment of the facilities requir
to sustain each group of sales. However, assuming the abov
is a reasonable approximation, it shows that in the long ter
the position is exactly reversed compared with the sho
term. Now it is the UK sales which are shown to be profitab
and the overseas sales are at break-even. The reason is th
the relevant cost of both the UK and the overseas sales
$$\frac{£100 + £50}{100} = £1·5.$$

10. The figure of £1·5 as the long-term relevant cost
confirmed if the position immediately after the acceptan
of the contract with Polski SA is reviewed. In that case U
sales are absorbing 50% of the capacity; the Polski contra
is absorbing 10% of the capacity and 40% of the capacity
unused and not therefore applicable to any of the curre
production; it is, in short, a management loss due to unde
utilization. The position could be shown thus:

	in thousands		
	UK	*overseas*	*total*
Contribution	£100·0	£10·0	£110·0
Less: fixed costs	50·0	10·0	60·0
Profit	£ 50·0	£—	£ 50·0
Less: unused facilities			40·0
			£ 10·0

11. The answer to the Managing Director's first question is therefore:

(a) In the short term £1 is the relevant cost

(b) In the long term £1·5 is the relevant cost

As to the dividing point between long and short term, it is the point after which the facilities represented by the fixed costs could be cancelled or applied to other remunerative purposes. This would, in practice, hardly be a point in time but rather a period of time.

The answer to the Managing Director's second question is that the correct basis for determining the price of the product is, first, to ascertain the acceptable range of prices in the market, and, secondly, to consider which price combined with the relevant turnover and the relevant costs will produce the greatest profit. On a long-term basis it would appear that home sales must be priced between £1·5 and the competitors' price of £1·75; it also appears that overseas sales are underpriced and are loss business, particularly as the strong demand suggests that the price could be raised.

Other applications of marginal costing

(a) MAKE OR BUY DECISIONS

Theorists advocate the use of marginal costing in solving make or buy problems. The idea is that the price payable to a supplier for, say, a component should be compared not with the total cost of making the item in the plant concerned, including a share of overheads, but with the marginal cost incurred by internal manufacture. The marginal cost in this case would consist probably of materials, labour and some element of variable expenses such as power. The trouble with this theory is that if it were put into effect it would probably show that there was no case where it was economic to buy out components; the reason being that the supplier's price would include his overheads and profit and thus always exceed the internal marginal cost.

In fact, manufacturers frequently do buy out components

which they could equally well have made within the plant,
and normally the reason is that by so doing the facilities are
freed for more vital manufacture. What this means, in effect
is that the facilities represented by the overheads applied to
the manufactured component can be applied more remuneratively to other purposes. Thus the cost of those
facilities is relevant to the manufacture of the component
and should be so applied for the purpose of comparison
with an outside supplier's price. In short the marginal cost is
not always the relevant cost.

(b) ALTERNATIVE METHODS OF PRODUCTION

Decisions under this title could embrace the use of alternative machines, transfers between manual and mechanical
methods, and the wider problem of the economics of complete automation of a process. Once again it is said that the
comparison between the alternatives should be made only
on the basis of the respective marginal costs. The proposition
has much force in such cases on the grounds that these
alternatives are normally unlikely to alter the fixed costs of
the plant or to make more facilities available for other
purposes. In the case of the use of alternative machines
there would be a case for treating as an opportunity cost the
profit foregone by using a particular machine where that
machine could be applied to other purposes. However, it is
by no means easy to assess the profitability of one element in
a lengthy production process and a more practical procedure
is to bring into the comparison an apportionment of the
replacement cost of each machine, as well as their respective
marginal operating costs.

(c) PROJECTS OF CAPITAL INVESTMENT

Marginal costs are particularly relevant in considering
projects of capital investment in, for instance, additional
machinery, the setting up of additional plants, and the
launching of new product lines. Since these are usually long
term projects depreciation is omitted and the cost of re-

lacing plant, etc, included as marginal costs. There could, however, be a case in particular circumstances for including n the calculations the cost of existing facilities which would e used by the new project.

7   Incentive Schemes

General considerations: advantages to employer and employee, various forms of schemes; Straight piecework; Time piecework; Effect of wages incentives on costs; The Halsey/Weir system; The Rowan system

General considerations

Incentive schemes may take a wide variety of forms an generally aim to induce the employees to provide more ou put in a given period of time than could otherwise be e pected in return for an effectively higher rate than their bas hourly remuneration. The advantage to the employer ca under suitable conditions, be twofold. Firstly, an increase i output per hour or week reduces unit costs by a greate spread of non-variable overheads (those independent c output in the short term). Secondly, and assuming th additional output can be sold, the normal profit per unit c sales is multiplied by a greater number of units sold in period.

The various forms of incentives operating in industry ma be broadly categorized as: (a) wage incentive schemes (wit which this section is largely concerned); and (b) other form of incentive not specifically related to the effort of individu workers or groups of workers. The latter may, for exampl take the form of profit-sharing schemes and fringe benefi such as superannuation, free insurance, sports and soci facilities, gratuities on marriage and generally attractiv working conditions. In general, all forms of incentive involv additional expense for a business so that, from a strict nancial viewpoint, their justification lies in the extent to which they reduce unit costs and/or increase output, i.e., the extent to which they produce more profit. It is, however, true that the same end has been achieved by forms of propaganda for encouraging economy or high output, such as by the setting of targets for individuals and teams and the fostering of company loyalty. These forms of incentive cost little more than the clerical and managerial effort involved but, in the present context, they merely represent the normal responsibility of management to achieve efficiency.

Wage incentive schemes may be generally classified as: a) pure piecework, i.e., a 'price' for each article produced, such as still exists for outworkers in the clothing industry; b) payment by time, i.e., where a straight hourly rate is paid and the worker can only increase his weekly or monthly take-home pay by working longer hours; or (c) a combination of piecework and time rates, this being the most interesting device from a costing viewpoint and probably the most widely used. A cross-section of the above categories is represented by those schemes which aim at the individual worker and those which concentrate on the team.

It is common knowledge that trade unions and local workers' representatives take a direct, often critical, but frequently constructive interest in the operation of incentive schemes. Their objectives may be said to be to ensure that the benefits of higher or more economical output are shared in some rational manner between workers and business. This desirable safeguard from the employees' position means that there is always a limit to which a wage incentive scheme alone can increase the profits of a business. It is only one device in the profit-earning process.

It also means that unless the arithmetic of the proposed incentive scheme is carefully worked out beforehand, the only party which gains may be the employee and the business loses profit as a result. The importance of this aspect of the matter is that once a scheme is instituted and agreed with workers' representatives it is very difficult to amend it so that the employees' benefits are reduced. An ill-considered scheme can thus become a burden and a commitment of long-term nature, much the same as the acceptance of period loan at an exorbitant rate of interest. It may als create conflict, which is sometimes said to have merits when it exists between members of the management team, but not known to increase productivity where it occurs between workers and management. For these reasons the nex section will attempt to examine the financial implications of some typical wage incentive schemes.

Straight piecework

Straight piecework may take the form either of a fixe payment for each article produced or the payment of a fixe hourly rate for an agreed time allowed for each article. Th former system has limited applications, e.g., to outworkers and the output obtainable from each worker is dependent on that worker's skill and requirement for remuneration Because of the effect of fatigue on marginal output there an obvious limit to the incentive effect of this type of scheme In general, if a business operating this scheme needs mor output it must either increase piece rates or find more out workers. The former will increase wage costs per unit of output, and the latter will increase overheads. The firs question for consideration in deciding on the merits of either alternative is whether the increase in overheads will be mor or less proportionate to the increase in output. Even if over heads rise to a higher rate per unit, an increase in piece rate to achieve higher output may, however, still be justified that increase remains below profit margins.

A simple illustration of the foregoing may not only b informative in relation to the somewhat rare case of pur piecework, but may also form a useful introduction to mor sophisticated forms of wage incentives.

Assume that in a given period 100 units of product ar normally produced by a certain number of workers at a pric per piece of £1; material costs are also £1 a unit; and over heads of £100 are incurred in processing the work. The situation may be considered as having reference to out-workers but could also apply, subject to a basic salary, to clerical staff, such as copy typists and machine operators.

Assume, further, that it is estimated that the workers would increase their output by 10% if they were paid at the rate of £1·20 per piece, and that the additional output would cause overheads to rise by £10. The comparative figures are as follows:

	existing situation	proposed situation
Output in units	100	110
Piecework rate	£1	£1·20
Labour cost	£100	£132
Material cost	100	110
Overhead cost	100	110
Total Costs	£300	£352
Cost per unit	£3·00	£3·20

The proposal is not justified on the basis of cost but could be justified if the profit margin is sufficient. In fact, on the figures given, a price obtainable for the product above £5·2 would justify the incentive scheme. It is pertinent to note that, with large amounts involved, interest on the additional funds required to finance the increase in turnover would need to be taken into account.

Like every management decision the above example is, in very elementary form, a problem of deciding between alternatives, the alternatives in this case being either to leave matters as they stand or to attempt to increase output by raising the wage rate. If the decision went against increasing the piecework rates the next problem for consideration might be whether to increase output by engaging more workers. The latter proposition might be worthwhile if the increase in output caused a less than proportionate increase in overheads. What was apparently a very simple problem has now become complex and involves the maximization of profit from the optimum relationship between piecework rates, turnover and movements in overheads, with the further complication of interest on the varying amounts of capital required and possibly discounts on material purchases. If it were found possible to obtain greater profit by raising output the further complicating factor could arise as to whether the increased output could be sold at the old price.

The conclusions to be drawn from this preliminary exercise may act as a guide to the appraisal of more complex incentive schemes, and may be summarized as follows:

1. It is first necessary to clarify the objectives of the incentive scheme: Is it aimed at producing more profit for the business? Is its objective limited to increasing output irrespective of profit aspects?

2. Wage incentive schemes will inevitably increase labour costs per unit so that any saving in costs must take the form of a reduction in overhead costs per unit which will probably (but not inevitably) follow an increase in output.

3. Even if an increase in output does not sufficiently reduce overhead costs per unit, the increased profit will arise if the product of the volume and the margin per unit increases.

4. Clarification of the limiting factors involved will help to reduce the scope of the exercise. The limiting factors will include: (a) the potential productivity of the workers, bearing in mind the factor of fatigue and the diminishing inducement of higher pay; (b) the physical constraints of the business, in the form of such matters as the space available, the capacity for processing the increased output, the funds available, etc; and (c) the

marketability of the increased volume of output, including considerations of price.

Time piecework or differential piecework

The expression 'time piecework' is used to embrace those schemes which are based on a combination of the time taken to complete a job and the 'price' payable for it. In all cases a basic wage is guaranteed whatever the time taken to complete the job. The other essential pre-requisite is for the time allowed to be accepted as fair by the workers or their representatives; in many cases schemes are agreed with trade unions for particular industries on a national basis. The time allowed is frequently calculated so as to ensure a bonus above normal hourly rates if only that time is achieved.

A fairly typical scheme is the Halsey or Weir system which allows the worker additional payment at his hourly rate on a proportion of the time he saves on the job, say one-half. Thus if the rate-fixed time allowed for a job was 30 hours, the time taken was 20 hours and the basic hourly rate was £1 an hour, the payment to the worker would be calculated as follows:

	hours
Time allowed	30
Time taken	20
Time saved	10
½ time saved	5

The worker would receive £1 (20 + 5) = £25

His actual rate of pay would be $£\dfrac{25}{20}$ = £1·25 per hour

This scheme ensures that a worker's rate of pay per hour increases as the time he saves rises, but the increase is not proportional or linear.

What are the implications for management of the Halsey/Weir system of wage incentive?

1. The decelerating effect of the bonus as the time saved increases, places an effective limit to the potential labour cost per hour, and thus to the dangers inherent in over-generous rate-fixing. This factor may also be presumed to place an effective limit on the improvement in output per hour which can be expected, because there will come a point when the reward obtainable from increasing his speed of work is no longer sufficiently attractive to the worker.

2. The fact that under this form of incentive scheme the rate of wages per job is always above that when plain time rates are paid, means for the business that there must be compensation in the form of lower overheads per job, and/or increased profit from the higher turnover.

3. The implication for costing is that the unit cost will be a quantity which can vary from time to time. Labour costs per unit will be high when bonus is high, and this situation is likely to exist when the order book is full and there is consequently pressure to obtain a high rate of output. Labour costs will tend to be low where the work load is known to be falling and the workers will have a natural inclination to slacken their efforts for fear of redundancy. There will thus be a tendency for labour costs to move in the reverse direction to that which is normally expected as a result of increasing or decreasing turnover.

4. Overheads, when expressed as an amount per unit of output, will tend to fall with high output, owing to the greater 'spread' of the non-variable element, and rise with low output – the opposite movement to that which is likely with labour costs. This is the short-term expectation; in the long term it is reasonable to assume that overheads will vary more or less directly in relation to output, and thus the unit cost of overheads is likely to remain reasonably static. This is, of course,

a very broad generalization and in considering the effect of an incentive scheme on overheads it will be wise to assume that increased indirect expenditure will be caused by the need for detailed rate-fixing, probably time and motion studies, and increased clerical work.

The effect of wage incentives on the use of costs

The question which is most pertinent for operating managers is the extent to which the introduction of a wage incentive scheme will affect the fulfilment of the objectives of costing. These objectives have already been summarized as: (a) the valuation of work in progress and stock; (b) guidance in the formulation of pricing policy; and (c) assistance in the managerial functions of forward planning and control.

The use of costs for valuing work in progress and stock will be complicated by the tendency suggested in the preceding section for changes in the rate of output to produce contrary movements in labour as compared with overhead costs per unit produced. The simple solution to this problem is to value stock on the basis of the normal situation, that is, to use standard costing. Likewise the effects on cost of an incentive scheme could produce anomalies in pricing policy if so-called 'actual costs' were used and, again, the remedy lies with the use of standard costing.

Somewhat different considerations apply to the use of cost figures by managers for planning and control purposes. Variances would remain an effective medium for initiating investigations into differences between the standard cost of production runs and the actual expenditure incurred. However, as indicated above, labour variances of both efficiency and rate could produce some unexpected figures and efforts to raise output to earn high premiums might cause increased rejects and material usage variances. If, in fact, the incentive scheme did result in a higher than normal rate of output, overhead recovery rates would need to be reviewed to accord with the new normal measure of capacity utilization.

Planning is largely a question of deciding between alternative courses of action and a common matter for consideration by management in this age of technological advance is whether to increase the mechanization or automation of the production processes. On the grounds that one of the primary objectives of increasing mechanization is to raise output, it is apparent that in considering the merits of such action, the relative merits of introducing an incentive scheme would be pertinent. Where an incentive scheme was already in operation and was causing high labour costs, the arguments for mechanization might be enhanced.

An example of the Halsey/Weir system

The effect of the Halsey/Weir system is shown by the following figures which presuppose that the number of man hours that can be generated in a workshop is limited; this limitation might be due, for instance, to restrictions on the space available.

Assume that 200,000 man hours can be generated in a workshop in a year; that the standard for each unit of production is 2 man hours; that the basic rate of pay is £1 an hour; that the overheads of the workshop are: variable £0·2 per unit produced, and fixed £100,000 in the year; and that material costs are £0·5 a unit. On average employees complete each job with a 20% saving on the standard time.

The questions for planning purposes are: (a) what is the likely output in a year? and (b) what is the probable unit cost? These problems may be solved on the following lines:

	in thousands
Actual man hours to be generated	200·0 hours
This represents 80% of the standard time which is therefore	250·0 hours
With a total time saved of	50·0 hours
the output at 2 units per hour of standard time is	500·0 units

The labour cost is

£1·0 (200 + 50/2)	=	£225·0
The material cost is £0·50 × 500·0 =		250·0

The overheads are:

non-variable	£100·0	
variable £0·2 × 500·0	100·0	
		200·0
Total expenditure		£675·0
Representing a unit cost of		£ 1·35

If it is further assumed that the price obtainable in the market for each unit is £2·00, the profit for the year becomes:

	in thousands
Sales: 500,000 @ £2	£1,000·0
Less: expenses, as above	675·0
Profit	£325·0

Now assume that the average time saved may be as low as 10%. The figures become:

	in thousands
Actual hours worked	200·0 hours
Standard hours generated	222·0 hours
Time saved	22·0 hours
Output	444·0 units

Labour cost: $£1·0 \left\{ 200·0 + \frac{22}{2} \right\}$		£211·0
Materials: £0·5 × 444·0		222·0

Overheads:

Non-variable	£100·0	
variable: £0·2 × 444	89·0	
		189·0
Total expenditure		£622·0

Representing a unit cost of		£1·4
Sales at 444·0 × £2 are	888·0	
	———	
Giving a profit of		£266·0

The following illustration is based on the assumption that the time saved will average 30%.

		in thousands
Actual hours worked		200·0 hours
Standard hours generated		286·0 hours
Time saved		86·0 hours
Output		572·0 units

Labour cost: £1·0 $\left\{200 + \dfrac{86}{2}\right\}$		£243·0
Materials: £0·50 × 572·0		286·0
Overheads:		
Non-variable	£100·0	
variable: £0·2 × 572·0	114·0	
	———	
	214·0	
	———	
Total expenditure		£743·0
Representing a unit cost of		£1·3
Sales at 572·0 × £2 are	£1144·0	
	———	
Giving a profit of		£401·0

The Rowan system

Another wage incentive of interest is the Rowan system which allows the worker, not a fixed percentage of the time saved as with the Halsey/Weir system, but that proportion of the time saved which the time taken bears to the time allowed. The bonus may thus be expressed as follows:

$$\text{Rate per hour} \times \left\{\frac{\text{time taken}}{\text{time allowed}} \times \text{time saved}\right\}$$

Applying this system to the original example the figures become:

Time allowed	30 hours
Time taken	20 hours
Time saved	10 hours

At the basic rate of £1 the worker would receive:

$$£1 \left(20 + \frac{20}{30} \times 10\right) = £26·67$$

It will be observed that with these figures the payment to the worker and therefore the cost of the job is somewhat higher than is the case with the Halsey/Weir system. Under the Rowan system the worker's hourly rate is better than that of the Halsey/Weir system up to the point when half the time allowed is saved and thereafter grows much less rapidly. The Rowan system consequently minimizes the cost to the business of gross errors in rate-fixing. The comparison is shown by the following table.

THE HALSEY AND ROWAN SYSTEMS OF INCENTIVE COMPARED

Time allowed: 30 hours   Basic hourly rate: £1

←	Halsey		→	←	Rowan		→
Time Taken	Time Saved	Pay-ment	Actual Hourly Rate	Time Taken	Time Saved	Pay-ment	Actual Hourly Rate
Hours	Hours	£	£	Hours	Hours	£	£
30	—	30·00	1·00	30	—	30·00	1·00
25	5	27·50	1·10	25	5	29·17	1·17
20	10	25·00	1·25	20	10	28·33	1·42
15	15	22·50	1·50	15	15	22·50	1·50
10	20	20·00	2·00	10	20	16·67	1·67
5	25	17·50	3·50	5	25	9·17	1·83

8 A Note on Replacement Costing

Replacement costs and the costing system; Accounting for replacement costs

Replacement costs and the costing system

Replacement costs essentially represent calculations to be made on an *ad hoc* basis, that is, when the need arises for a particular purpose in relation to a product or a service. The cost of replacing a stock of materials or components will vary from time to time in relation to circumstances external to the business, rises in prices and changes in technology. For this reason it would be difficult to construct a costing system which was designed to produce replacement costs as a matter of routine, although such systems are in existence. In any event, as argued in the preceding chapter, the costing *system* in a modern business has its essential justification of arriving at the value of stocks and work in progress, for which purpose, in order to conform to the rule of consistency, it is necessary to apply a set of conventions. The two concepts of cost most frequently applied to a costing system used to value stocks and work in progress are either: (a) historical costs; or (b) standard costs. In this application of costing the objective is to formulate a valuation of stocks and work in progress which, because valuation is the essence of profit ascertainment, should be designed to produce a view of profit which will be consistent and thus comparable from year to year. It is arguable that a convention which used replacement costs, with its inevitable variations from time to time, would not apparently produce consistency or comparability of business results from period to period. Another objection is that replacement costing as a system would apparently involve a substantial increase in administrative effort, if only in ascertaining what in fact was the replacement cost of every item of material and every kind of service purchased by the business.

On the assumption that a costing *system* is primarily designed as an element in the process of profit ascertainment, the essential justification for using such a system with that end in view would be that: (a) it produced a more realistic view of the capital employed in the business; and hence (b) it showed a realistic view of the profit made or loss suffered in a period. Profit in accounting terms is simply the increase in capital employed, after eliminating additional capital and withdrawals of capital and profit.

If, therefore, in using replacement costing the effect was that stocks were valued at replacement cost, and replacement cost was greater than historical cost – a common situation in these times – then the stocks and hence the capital employed in the business would be valued at a higher figure than if historical cost were used. One would expect in consequence that profit would be commensurately higher than would be the case with a historical costing system, but this reasonable consequence will not in fact occur. What the accounts will show is that the profit on sales will be lower with a replacement costing system than with a historical costing system, the reason being that a higher cost will be set against the sales made. It is true that the net assets of the concern will be higher because a notional profit will be shown on the stock. This profit would not, however, normally be shown in the profit and loss account but would be added to reserve, probably a special reserve created for the purpose.

Accounting for replacement costs

The accounting process may be illustrated by the following simplified example.

Imagine a business beginning a year with a capital of £50,000 consisting entirely of 10,000 units of finished stock acquired at a cost of £5 each. Assume that during the year 6,000 of these units were sold at a price of £10 each and the sales were paid for in cash. With a historical costing system the year end profit and loss account and balance sheet would appear as follows:

PROFIT AND LOSS ACCOUNT

Sales – 6,000 @ £10	£60,000
Less: cost of goods sold – 6,000 @ £5	£30,000
Profit	£30,000

BALANCE SHEET

Capital employed

Original capital	£50,000
Profit	£30,000
	£80,000

represented by:

Stock – 4,000 @ £5	£20,000
Cash (from sales)	£60,000
	£80,000

Now assume that the replacement cost of the stock was £6 and the stock remaining was valued at that figure. The statements would appear as follows:

PROFIT AND LOSS ACCOUNT

Sales – 6,000 @ £10	£60,000
Less: cost of goods sold – 6,000 @ £6	£36,000
Profit	£24,000

BALANCE SHEET

Capital employed	
Original capital	£50,000
Reserve (increase in value of original stock of 10,000 units at £1)	£10,000
Profit	£24,000
	£84,000

represented by:	
Stock – 4,000 @ £6	£24,000
Cash (from sales)	£60,000
	£84,000

With the historical cost method the percentage profit on capital at the beginning was 60% and in the second case was 48%. The percentages on average capital are 46% and 36%. In other words, with the above version of a replacement costing system in operation distributable profit will be very much below that with a historical costing system, both in amount and as a percentage; but in the latter case the shareholders' interest will be shown to have increased substantially.

What has been achieved by the latter form of presentation of the results is apparently as follows:

(a) Whereas in the first and traditional form of presentation the shareholders' interest in the concern is shown as original cost, i.e., the amount of money actually in the bank or the till plus the money paid for the remaining stock; in the second, replacement cost form of presentation, the stock is shown at the higher replacement cost, i.e., nearer present values but still not in terms of saleable value. The result is that the book value per share is shown to have increased from $£\frac{80}{50} = £1\cdot6$ to $£\frac{84}{50} = £1\cdot68$. Whether this change means anything in particular to the shareholder is doubtful, for the real value of the share is neither one nor the other figure but the amount which it will fetch in the market at a particular point of time.

(b) What has occurred to the presentation of profit? The answer to this question must depend on the individual's conception of the meaning of the word 'profit' which, like many familiar expressions, is an imprecise term. It is largely dependent on the basis on which the assets and liabilities of the business are valued; and value depends on the point of view. If profit is regarded as the amount available for distribution (e.g., as dividends) without impairing the earning value of the capital, then it is clear from the above example that a replacement system of costing would, in a period of rising prices, reduce the distributable profit. The validity of the idea that profit is the balance of funds remaining after the cost of replacing stock has been set off against sales income arises from the supposed fact that a business cannot continue indefinitely unless it continually replaces its stock. The qualifications to this idea are (a) that in a changing economy the stock replaced is not often the same as the stock used; and (b) if business is looked upon as a series of disparate ventures, then it is in fact continually being wound up and beginning again; in which case it is the original cost of the stock which is appropriate to the exercise of profit ascertainment and the capital for the next venture must be found out of past profits.

(c) Perhaps the more forceful, although pragmatic, justification for the replacement system of costing is that, in a period of rising prices, it enforces the retention of a portion of the profits in the business, so that the funds are available for the activities of the next period. The same result could be achieved if the directors limited the dividends payable out of the higher profits shown by a more traditional method of accounting. This is undoubtedly the practice of many boards of directors, but in so doing it would be quite natural for them to consider the likely reaction of the shareholders, whose power lies in their ability to vote the directors in and out of office. The influence of human nature on accounting presentations may be logically unjustifiable but it is practically unavoidable. The business world impatiently awaits the formulation of a generally accepted accounting convention which will indicate how much of the year's profit is available for distribution.

(d) Another important consequence of a replacement system of accounting is that the figures so produced can be used for a variety of purposes. As stated above a costing *system* is basically necessary for the valuation of stock and work in progress, as an integral part of the accounting mechanics of preparing profit and loss accounts and balance sheets. If, as argued previously, the replacement cost is superior in many situations to the historical cost for management decisions and as an aid to pricing policy, then the same figures can be used for all these purposes. The administrative difficulty is, however, that the true cost of replacing a particular resource used in business, whether material, machinery or a service, is difficult to ascertain and changes from time to time. Thus even a replacement system of costing will inevitably be forced into the adoption of conventions in the interests of the economy and practicability of accounting; and will, accordingly, represent qualified truth.

In considering the validity of the replacement approach to costing it should be borne in mind that much of the preceding discussion presupposed rising prices. This supposition is generally justified by the concern which is widely expressed about inflation in modern times. However, even in a general era of inflation, the price of many products and services has fallen, at least temporarily. To the extent that the cost of materials, machinery and services falls, so will the price of manufactured products tend to fall. If a replacement system of costing is used when there is a substantial fall in prices, then the consequence on profit outlined above will be reversed. Such a situation is quite conceivable where material costs which form a large element of total costs are falling. With replacement costing the distributable profit will be higher than that shown by a historical costing system, but the fall in value of the remaining stock will cause a reduction rather than an increase in reserves. More probably the reduction in stock values would be written off as an exceptional item direct to profit and loss account and the resulting picture may be illustrated as follows:

Assume the same facts as in the foregoing example except that instead of rising to £6 a unit, the replacement cost of the stock has fallen to £4 a unit.

PROFIT AND LOSS ACCOUNT

Sales – 6,000 @ £10	£60,000
Less: cost of goods sold – 6,000 @ £4	£24,000
Profit so far	£36,000
Less: loss on stock – 10,000 @ £1	£10,000
Final Profit	£26,000

BALANCE SHEET

Capital Employed

Original capital	£50,000
Profit	£26,000
	£76,000

Represented by:

Stock – 4,000 @ £4	£16,000
Receipts from sales	£60,000
	£76,000

It is important that the art and science of accounting should be based upon a body of reasonable, adaptable and widely recognized rules; it is equally important that its presentations

hould show the information which is required by the
managers and the owners of the business, as well as to the
general public and other interested parties. The following
final set of accounts is therefore set out, not as the desirable
answer to the problem, but merely as indicating that accounting can be adapted to show the information that the
management require.

Suppose, therefore, that the management wish to see: (a)
what profit has resulted after charging sales with the replacement cost of stock used; and (b) the financial position on the
basis of the money expended to buy the assets. Reverting,
now, to the situation where the historical cost of the stock
was £5 and its replacement cost was £6, the statements *could*
be drawn up on the following lines:

PROFIT AND LOSS ACCOUNT

Sales – 6,000 @ £10	£60,000
Less: cost of goods sold at replacement cost, i.e., 6,000 @ £6	£36,000
	£24,000

BALANCE SHEET

Capital Employed

Original capital	£50,000
Profit (distributable)	£24,000
Reserve (inflation profit on stock sold)	£ 6,000
	£80,000

Represented by:

Stock at original cost – 4,000 @ £5	£20,000
Cash from sales	£60,000
	£80,000

So we have three distinct pictures of the results of trading over the period, each of them having a justification in reason, each of them showing substantially different views of cost and profit. Which of these pictures shows the truth? The answer to that question is, it is suggested, that they are all true. ' "Everybody has won and all must have prizes," said the Dodo.' The real question is: What does the management wish to know in order to plan and control the business? So far as cost is concerned, it has already been suggested that the information required by management must depend on the particular purposes in mind, and because of the variety of purposes which need to be considered from time to time in business, there is no one absolute figure of the cost of a service, operation or product which is applicable to all purposes.

So far as the presentation of profit is concerned, different considerations apply. Because profit depends on value, which is a point of view, and because its presentation needs to be consistent and comparable from period to period (if not from business to business), it is necessary that widely recognized conventions should be adopted. Whilst there is considerable controversy about the validity of some of the conventions currently in use, and considerable variations between one organization and another, it is somewhat boldly suggested that the adoption of replacement costing *as a system* is hardly likely to clarify the picture, for the reasons given above.

It is interesting to observe that in 1971 the Phillips organization, which had been using a somewhat sophisticated system of replacement costing and accounting for many years, decided to modify the system. The reason given was that it tended to show too small profits. No doubt the decision to modify the system was influenced by the persistent inflation of prices in recent years. If any generally applicable conclusion can be drawn from the modification in the accounting system of this enormous organization, it is that costing and accounting must be adapted to circumstances. The conclusion will undoubtedly offend the theorists;

so will the further conclusion that, provided its limitations are understood, there is still much to be said on the grounds of consistency for the historical costing system.

Index

Financial and Managerial Accounting by H. Bierman (Mac
millan, NY). An expansive but readable American boo
which combines practicality with sound theory.

Business Planning by D. R. C. Halford (Pan Books Lt
Management Series). An interesting book with a stro
leaning towards marginal or direct costing and of particul
interest to those conversant with mathematical technique

BIBLIOGRAPHY

Finance and Accounts for Managers by Desmond Goch (Pan Books Ltd, Management Series). This is a simply expressed but comprehensive guide to the financial and accounting function in business and would be useful reading for the manager without an accounting background.

Financial Planning and Control by A. H. Taylor and R. E. Palmer (Pan Books Ltd, Management Series). This is also a book written primarily for managers without detailed accounting knowledge and develops the financial aspects of forward planning and control in business, including budgetary control.

Studies in Costing by D. Solomon (Sweet and Maxwell). A well-established book which examines various costing practices in a logical manner and requires no expert knowledge for a general understanding.

Cost Accounting: A Managerial Emphasis by C. T. Horngren (Prentice Hall). A well-written American book which covers management accounting and costing in considerable depth and would be useful for reference to those who wish to study particular aspects of the subject.

Standard Costing by J. Batty (Macdonald and Evans). A useful textbook for reference on the technique of standard costing.

Financial and Cost Accounting for Management by Taylor and Shearing (Macdonald and Evans). A fairly wide-ranging book for managers, which covers the subjects indicated by the title.

Financing Business and Industry by R. Drew Carran (Pan Books Ltd, Management Series). A further development of the subject for the manager, emphasizing the sourcing and control of funds and with a particularly clear chapter on the appraisal of new capital projects.

INDEX

Peter F. Drucker

TECHNOLOGY, MANAGEMENT AND SOCIETY   45p

In this volume the author has collected twelve essays on technology and management with their relationship to, and interaction with, human society.

In these essays the reader is able to grasp and savour some of the essential ideas and philosophy that have been expanded into Peter Drucker's various books.

THE AGE OF DISCONTINUITY   60p

Peter Drucker focuses with great clarity and perception on the new forces that are creating tomorrow's society. These are the forces of discontinuity in our social, political, and economic landscape. The essential question is 'what must we do today to shape tomorrow?'

Peter F. Drucker

MANAGING FOR RESULTS 50p

'This is the sort of book that the lively business-man likes. It's unashamed aim is the increase of profits. Where it scores is in quoting actual case histories from such companies as General Motors, Philips, American General Electric and IBM' – ACHIEVEMENT

THE PRACTICE OF MANAGEMENT 60p

'Peter Drucker has three outstanding gifts as a writer on business – acute perception, brilliant skill as a reporter and unlimited self-confidence . . . His penetrating accounts of the Ford Company, the retail enterprise of Sears Roebuck, and, most interesting of all, the International Business Machines concern, are worth a library of formal business histories'
– NEW STATESMAN

Graham Turner

'The most dramatic industrial story that can possibly have been written' – LORD ROBENS

THE LEYLAND PAPERS   60p

'It is the story of thwarted ambitions and industrial savagery ... the story of a human catalyst of all that is good and bad in the tough jungle of the business world, of political intervention, of secret meetings and corridor discussions that finally gave birth to the second largest motor manufacturer outside the States' – THE SPECTATOR

'Graham Turner pulls no punches ... eminently readable, a vital contribution to British Industrial history' – BOOKS AND BOOKMEN

Goronwy Rees

'. . . we both felt that making people happy was the great thing in life' – LORD SIEFF

ST MICHAEL
A History of Marks & Spencer   60p

'The story of Marks and Spencer's success. It is one of consistent efforts to provide high quality goods at low price, inspired by the partnership of Lord Marks and Lord Sieff, whose philosophy has made the firm unique among British business institutions' – SUNDAY TELEGRAPH